Dismissal of Tenured Higher Education Faculty: Legal Implications of the Elimination of Mandatory Retirement

Arval A. Morris
Professor of Law
Adjunct Professor of Education
University of Washington

DISCLAIMER

The National Organization on Legal Problems of Education (NOLPE) is a private, nonadvocacy, and nonprofit association of educators and attorneys. The opinions expressed in this publication are those of the author and do not represent official views of the Organization.

Published by

NATIONAL ORGANIZATION ON LEGAL PROBLEMS OF EDUCATION
3601 S.W. 29th Street, Suite 223
Topeka, Kansas 66614
(913) 273-3550

TABLE OF CONTENTS

I. INTRODUCTION

A. Description of the Age Discrimination in Employment Act

American national policy is clearly that of prohibiting age discrimination in employment, including age-based mandatory retirement. In 1967, Congress enacted the Age Discrimination in Employment Act[1] (ADEA), which became effective June, 1968,[2] and which prohibited age discrimination in employment against persons between the ages of 40 and 65. The law was amended in 1974 to expand the definition of "employer" to include "state and local governments."[3] In 1977, a U.S. Supreme Court decision interpreted the ADEA to permit employers to force employees within the ADEA's then protected age group (40 to 65) to retire involuntarily, so long as the employers' action was not a subterfuge designed to avoid the ADEA and to fire older workers which meant that the employer's action must be taken pursuant to an otherwise *bona fide* retirement system.[4] Congress, in 1978, immediately responded to the decision. It repudiated and changed the Supreme Court's interpretation of the law by enacting amendments to the ADEA, making it clear that the ADEA was not to be circumvented and that involuntary terminations of covered employees by an employer even when accomplished pursuant to a *bona fide* retirement plan, are to be treated under the Act just like any other involuntary termination of employment, except for mandatory retirement of a narrowly defined group of "bona fide executive[s]

---

[1] 29 U.S.C. §§ 621-34

[2] *See*, EEOC v. Wyoming, 460 U.S. 226 (1983)

[3] EEOC v. Wyoming, 460 U.S. 226, 229 (1983). The 1974 amendments are virtually identical to the approach of the 1972 amendments to Title VII of the Civil Rights Act of 1964 which prohibits discrimination in employment based on race, sex, religion or national origin. The constitutionality of applying the ADEA to states and to their political subdivisions as an exercise of Congress' authority under the Commerce Clause and the Fourteenth Amendment was upheld by the Supreme Court of the United States in EEOC v. Wyoming, 460 U.S. 226 1983); also *see*, Garcia v. San Antonio, 469 U.S. 528 (1985). The 1974 amendments prescribe separate procedures for resolutions of complaints by federal employees. The ADEA now covers employers who have 20 or more employees, labor unions with 25 members, and employment agencies. The Older American Act Amendments of 1984 specifically protect all U.S. Citizens "employed by an employer in a workplace in a foreign country," but this protection is qualified where "compliance with [the ADEA] would cause such employer to violate the laws of the country in which the workplace is located." 29 U.S.C. § 623(g). At a minimum, the 1984 Act covers U.S. Citizen employees working in a foreign country for American corporations and their subsidiaries. The Age Discrimination Act of 1975, as amended, 42 U.S.C. § 6101 *et seq.*, prohibits discrimination at any age in programs or activities receiving federal financial assistance.

[4] United Air Lines, Inc. v. McMann, 434 U.S. 192 (1977).

or high policymaker[s]"[5] who have vested retirement benefits over a statutorily required dollar amount. The 1978 amendments also expanded federal protection against age discrimination from age 65 to 70, making the protected age group 40 to 70.[6]

In Autumn 1986, Congress significantly changed the ADEA by enacting additional amendments that, with few exceptions, effectively prohibit age-based mandatory retirement policies in almost all areas of American employment.[7] Congress achieved this end by simply removing the ADEA's age-70 cap on the class of protected employees effective January 1, 1987.[8] Section 12(a) of the ADEA now reads: "The prohibitions of this Act shall be limited to individuals who are at least 40 years of age."[9] Therefore, today, and with very few exceptions identified below, almost everyone in the United States over the age of 40 is protected by the ADEA or a comparable state law. As covered by the ADEA, employers may not now discriminate on the basis of age when hiring, nor, except as otherwise allowed by the Act, involuntarily retire any person over 40 simply because of age. Persons within the protected class; i.e., over the age of 40, can be severed from their employment only because of deficient performance or for other legitimate business or organizational reasons, but not because of the arrival of a particular birthday.

Currently, there are four limited exceptions to the rule prohibiting employers from enforcing mandatory-age retirement policies. One — corporate executives or high policy makers — has already been identified.[10] A second exception is a general category exception permitting any employer

---

[5] 29 U.S.C. § 631(c). Federal regulations narrowly construe this exemption from the ADEA. 29 C.F.R. § 1625.12. "Bona fide executive" status applies "only to a very few top level employees who exercise substantial executive authority over a significant number of employees and a large volume of business," such as heads major corporate divisions of corporate headquarters. Id. § 1625(d)(2). "High policy making" status is restricted to "certain top level employees ... whose position and responsibility are such that they play a significant role in the development of corporate policy and effectively recommend the implementation thereof, ... ". Id. § 1625.12(e), quoting H.R. Rep. 950, 95th Cong., 2nd Sess. 10 (1978).

[6] Pub. Law 95-256, § 3(a); 92 Stat. 189, 190; 29 U.S.C. § 631 (1978). Congress soon amended the ADEA twice more — in 1982 through the Tax Equity and Fiscal Responsibility Act (96 Stat. 324, 353) making it difficult for employers to transfer their burden for medical insurance of their employees over 65 to the financially troubled Medicare-Medicaid programs, and again in 1984 as part of the Deficit Reduction Act (98 Stat. 1036), further clarifying employers' obligations under the 1982 amendment regarding employer responsibilities for health care benefits to spouses of employees.

[7] Similar laws have been passed by the states covering most employers not subject to the ADEA such that, today, age-based mandatory retirement policies are generally prohibited throughout the United States.

[8] An exception to the amendment going into effect on January 1, 1987, involved collective bargaining contracts containing age-70 mandatory retirement provisions, which were permitted to continue in force until the expiration of the agreement or January 1, 1990, whichever occurred first.

[9] 29 U.S.C. § 631a.

[10] *See* text at footnote 5, *supra*.

to use age as a criterion whenever an employer can demonstrate that age constitutes a Bona Fide Occupational Qualification (BFOQ) because the ADEA permits an employer "to take any action otherwise prohibited [by the Act] . . . where age is a *bona fide* occupational qualification reasonably necessary to the normal operation of the particular business."[11] The BFOQ is an employer defense, and according to the EEOC it is to "have limited scope and application" and must be "narrowly construed."[12] A United States Supreme Court decision upholds the EEOC's approach to BFOQs in a case in which the Court sustained a jury verdict that age 60 was not a general BFOQ for retirement of commercial airlines flight engineers, signalling that individualized decisions about an individual's personal capacities, skills, experience and performance must be made in each case.[13]

In its 1986 amendments to the ADEA, Congress provided two additional but temporary exceptions to the rule prohibiting mandatory age retirement. Until midnight, December 31, 1993, it permitted "states and their political subdivisions" to discharge or to refuse to hire firefighters or law enforcement

---

[11] 29 U.S.C. § 623(f)(1).

[12] 29 C.F.R. § 1625.6(a). Thus, to be in compliance with 29 C.F.R. §1625.6(b):

   An employer asserting a BFOQ defense has the burden of proving that (1) the age limit is reasonably necessary to the essence of the business, and either (2) that all or substantially all individuals excluded from the job involved are in fact disqualified, or (3) that some of the individuals so excluded possess a disqualifying trait that cannot be ascertained except by reference to age. If the employer's objective in asserting a BFOQ is the goal of public safety, the employer must prove that the challenged practice does indeed effectuate that goal and that there is no acceptable alternative which would better advance it or equally advance it with less discriminatory impact.

[13] Western Air Lines v. Criswell, 472 U.S. 400 (1985). On the other hand, a court of appeals case, decided before *Criswell* and before Congress's 1986 Amendments to the ADEA and not reviewed by the U.S. Supreme Court, seems to be an exception to the ADEA's requirement of individualization and allows an age-based BFOQ. In Hodgson v. Greyhound Lines, 499 F.2d 859 (7th Cir. 1974), *cert. denied*, 419 U.S. 1122 (1974), the employer justified using a 35 year age cut-off as a BFOQ for hiring drivers by presenting evidence that average safety records improved with 15 to 20 years experience, but began to decline on the average after age 55. The employer argued successfully that it could not receive the organizational benefits from driver experience if it hired drivers over the age of 40 and then waited until they reached 55 to determine which of them might be exceptions to the average. Conceivably, this approach, if ultimately approved by the Supreme Court, might be applied to older employees having industrial jobs with respect to safety; *see*, Mitchell, *The Relation of Age to Workplace Injuries*, MONTHLY LABOR REV. (July, 1988), at 8 ff. (workers over 65 are more likely to suffer permanent disabilities, but job risk patterns do not very with age regarding temporary disabilities).

   It is highly unlikely courts will rule that age in a college or university context is a BFOQ. Increasing age may be related to declining physical ability, but not necessarily to certain kinds of intellectual activity. "Crystallized intelligence" is the ability to make use of an accumulated body of general information for making judgments and solving problems, and may continue to rise over the entire life span of active, healthy people. But creative "fluid intelligence" — the capacity to manipulate abstract relationships and patterns creatively — may begin to decline in the mid-70s for most people, although there have been spectacular exceptions; e.g. Verdi's operatic creativity after age 70. *See*, *e.g.*, Goleman, *The Aging Mind Proves Capable of Lifelong Growth*, N.Y. Times, Feb. 21, 1984, Sec. C, p. 1, col. 3, summarizing research.

officers on *bona fide* grounds if the action is taken pursuant to a state or local law effective as of March 3, 1983, and if the individual has attained the age for retirement (or against hiring) prescribed in the law.[14] Congress provided its fourth exception with respect to tenured professors in higher education. It permitted existing, compulsory retirement-age policies to be applied to employees by their college or university employer at age 70 if the employees are "serving under a contract of unlimited tenure . . . at an institution of higher education."[15] This last provision also will expire automatically at midnight on December 31, 1993. The 1986 amendments further require that the EEOC commission the National Academy of Sciences to study (and to report on) the potential consequences of the elimination of mandatory-age retirement policies on institutions of higher education.

B. Overview of the Study

The conceptual, legal and related aspects of tenure involved in the termination of the fourth exception to the ADEA is the subject of this Study. It focuses first in Part II on the concept of tenure, itself, and on its function and justification, without considering the law because of the existence of considerable confusion and misunderstanding of the concept of tenure and its role in higher education. A clear understanding of the concept of tenure, its function in higher education and its flexibility are necessary before one can assess tenure's potential role in the totality of the consequences, if any, for institutions of higher education because of the ADEA's elimination of mandatory-age retirement policies. If the concept of tenure is, itself, a rigid, inflexible and insurmountable barrier to institutions such that it precludes or materially impairs them from removing tenured faculty members of all ages who are of demonstrated professional incompetency or dishonest, or those who substantially and manifestly neglect their professional duties, then the concept of tenure will be a formidable obstacle indeed when it is implemented by the law because, in essence, it would guarantee lifetime employment irrespective of performance. On the other hand, if the concept of tenure is flexible, constituting no genuine barrier to removal of faculty members who are demonstrably deficient in their professional competencies or re-

---

[14] 29 U.S.C. § 623(i). Apparently, this situation is a response to Johnson v. Baltimore, 472 U.S. 353 (1985), in which the Supreme Court struck down mandatory retirement for firefighters at age 55, although federal firefighters and police could be retired at that age. Congress, in the 1986 amendments, directed the Secretary of Labor and the EEOC to conduct a study and to report to Congress on this situation by January 1, 1991, especially with respect to the reliability and probative value of various tests measuring physical and mental fitness that could be used in firefighter and police officer selection.

[15] 29 U.S.C. § 631(d).

sponsibilities, and if the concept of tenure has for its goal the creation of a necessary foundation which materially aids institutions of higher learning to achieve their educational goals, then the concept of academic tenure not only aids institutions of higher education to achieve their educational goals, but also, it neither precludes them, nor materially impairs them from realizing their educational goals. If the latter view accurately describes the concept of tenure, and if the law that implements the concept of tenure is itself, faithful to that concept (which is discussed in Part III of this Study), then neither the concept of tenure nor its legal implementation would constitute a disabling barrier precluding or materially impairing institutions of higher education from realizing their educational goals. If this latter situation is true, then the institution of academic tenure as a whole constitutes no significant impediment to the ADEA's elimination of mandatory-age retirement policies of higher education institutions.

After Part II's analysis of the concept of tenure, Part III of this Study generally addresses the legal aspects of the question whether the concept of academic tenure, as implemented by the law, and if continued beyond age 70 for tenured faculty members, collectively constitutes an unacceptable obstacle for institutions of higher education such that their efforts to achieve their educational goals would be unacceptably impaired if mandatory-age retirement policies are prohibited by the ADEA. The focus of Part III necessarily must be on the law, and particularly on whether institutions of higher education reasonably have the legal ability to dismiss tenured faculty members of any age who lapse into "demonstrated incompetence or dishonesty," or "substantial and manifest neglect of duty."

It must be clearly recognized that in an age-uncapped context, the legal dimensions of tenure can constitute an unacceptable obstacle for institutions of higher education precluding, or insurmountably hindering, them from reaching their educational goals *only* if *two* conditions are fully satisfied:

(1) that the institution of academic tenure generally does, in legal fact and because of the law's general rules, unacceptably and unreasonably protect from dismissal or other appropriate sanctions tenured faculty members of either demonstrated professional incompetence or dishonesty, or those who substantially and manifestly neglect their professional duties, and

(2) that after uncapping occurs, the number of tenured faculty members beyond the age of 70 who do not voluntarily retire will be very large, of which a very large proportion will lapse into demonstrated incompetence or dishonesty, or substantial and manifest neglect of professional duties, making unacceptable the total number of tenured faculty members who annually fall into both categories and cannot be readily dismissed because of the law.

An exploration of the second condition is, an empirical prediction beyond the scope of this Study, and is not pursued here. Part III of the Study concentrates its discussion on the first necessary condition. Its focus is on the role of law involved in the involuntary removal of tenure from faculty members previously holding it, and this focus necessarily involves a discussion of legal cases. They should be considered as examples of legal precedent that will be applied in analogous situations.

But, it should be clearly recognized, as especially identified by the recommendation at the end of Part III, that the involuntary removal of tenure and dismissal of a faculty member involves much, much more than the law. In this situation, the wise and humane use of legal doctrines by college or university authorities, just as in other situations, will usually make all the difference between a dignified and mutually beneficial faculty retirement and an acrimonious tenure hearing at the institution perhaps followed by a lawsuit, after which it usually is impossible to say that anyone "won" in the broader, academic sense, irrespective of the legal outcome of the case. To reach the proper salubrious end, every institution of higher learning should have in place a set of precisely stated procedures that afford full due process, plus a pre-dismissal procedure similar to that recommended at the end of Part III. Constituent elements of necessary procedures will be suggested throughout Parts II and III of this Study.

Because of the Study's perspective in Part III, not all cases involving the involuntary dismissal of tenured faculty members will be considered. This Study concentrates primarily on those cases involving the involuntary dismissal of tenured faculty members on grounds such as "demonstrated incompetence or dishonesty," or "substantial and manifest neglect of duty" (the latter ground properly includes "insubordination," although many institutions provide for both grounds separately in their faculty codes, with either serving as an independent ground for the dismissal of tenured faculty members), rather than on cases of involuntary removal of tenure on essentially "moral" grounds. The reason for the Study's primary concentration on cases concerning "demonstrated incompetence or dishonesty" or "substantial and manifest neglect of duty" including "insubordination," as grounds for the involuntary dismissal of tenured faculty members is the belief that these cases reveal more fundamentally, than do the cases involving "moral" grounds, the critical relationship existing between the legal dimensions of tenure and its effects, if any, which are relevant to considerations of the ADEA's elimination of mandatory-age retirement policies beyond the age of seventy for tenured faculty members. This Study assumes there will be no significant increase in "moral" offense cases involving tenured faculty members over the age of 70 that would materially hinder institutions of higher education from achieving their educational goals if the ADE prohibits colleges and universities from applying mandatory-age retirement policies to tenured faculty members when they reach their seventieth birthday.

II. THE CONCEPT OF TENURE

A. Misconceptions

Misconceptions of the concept of academic tenure for faculty members at institutions of higher learning are commonplace; so much so that ignorance of, or hostility to, tenure unexpectedly has appeared in high places. For example, South Dakota's Supreme Court ruled that a tenure policy, which prevented a state college's board of regents from dismissing a tenured faculty member without first obtaining the approval of the president of the college and of the faculty tenure committee constituted "such delegation of [board of regent] authority to subordinates [that it] is an unlawful encroachment upon the board of regents' constitutional and statutory power of control over such college."[16] In the course of his opinion for the State Supreme Court, Judge Hanson solemnly declared that "the exact meaning and intent of this so-called tenure policy eludes us. Its vaporous objectives, purposes, and procedures are lost in a fog of nebulous verbiage." Cases like this one contrast sharply with the widespread but fallacious view that the concept of tenure as implemented by rules of law weld faculty members forever to their tenured university or college positions.

B. The Fundamental Function of Academic Tenure

Proponents argue that academic tenure guarantees the very foundation of intellectual freedom so necessary to the creativity and rigor of America's colleges and universities.[17] In this view, tenure provides crucially important but often neglected and overlooked benefits for the common good of American society as a whole. The point has been pithily stated by C. Byse and L. Joughin:[18]

---

[16] Worzella v. Board of Regents, 93 N.W.2d 411, 414 (S.D. 1958). For commentary *see*, C. Byse, *Academic Freedom and the Law: A Comment on Worzella v. Board of Regents*, 73 HARV. L. REV. 304 (1959).

[17] For the history of academic freedom *see*, R. Hofstadter & W. Metzger, THE DEVELOPMENT OF ACADEMIC FREEDOM IN THE UNITED STATES (1955).

[18] Clark Byse and Louis Joughin, TENURE IN AMERICAN HIGHER EDUCATION: PLANS, PRACTICES AND THE LAW p. 4 (1959).

> Academic freedom and tenure do not exist because of a peculiar solicitude for the human beings who staff our academic institutions. They exist, instead, in order that society may have the benefit of honest judgment and independent criticism which otherwise might be withheld because of fear of offending a dominant social group or transient social attitude.

The primary benefit the institution of faculty tenure provides to American society lies in its vigorous protection of academic freedom[19] which, when collectively exercised by all faculty members, generates: (1) a continuing beneficial flow into society of an enormously wide range of creatively new knowledge that, in turn, generates useful social and physical innovations; (2) an equal flow of criticism that refines existing useful ideas and discards others; and additionally, (3) tenure and academic freedom provide the foundation assuring that faculty members might progressively revise and upgrade the ways in which they educate and train people who thereby become more effectively competent in a wide variety of skills and methods, and who are then able to help their communities, states and nations by acting effectively when discharging a vast spectrum of social roles. Professional scholarship is the key. Scholarship surely means the discovery of knowledge through research. But scholarship also means the refinement and integration of knowledge into a coherent structure; the precise and efficient application of knowledge; and of extreme importance, the presentation of knowledge, as in great teaching. Consequently, the greatest part of all the benefits derived from scholars collectively and vigorously exercising their freedom to inquire, speak, meet, teach and publish does not accrue directly to them, but to millions of their contemporary human beings in the United States and elsewhere, and to millions in posterity. Without such a flow of newly created or subsequently refined knowledge, creative innovations, and skillfully trained people, American society would stagnate.

The fundamental function of academic tenure is directly to protect academic freedom. The societal benefits provided by academic freedom and tenure occur because of the belief that the tenured scholar should receive tenure's protections whenever he or she professionally exercises academic freedom, for example, by uninhibitedly criticizing or advocating changes: (1) of any accepted or newly new-emerging theory, method, skill, or practice; (2) of widely held social beliefs, and social or governmental policies; (3) of existing social, political, legal or economic institutions; (4) of the policies and programs of the educational institution served by the faculty member,

---

[19]   For discussion see, E. Pincoffs (ed.), THE CONCEPT OF ACADEMIC FREEDOM (1972).

including its administration and governing board; and in addition (5) by coming to the aid of any colleagues whose academic freedom is in jeopardy.[20]

Although the two concepts of tenure and academic freedom can be separated conceptually and treated independently, they are intertwined, fundamentally informing each other, and mutual reinforcing because both focus on fully encouraging and protecting the fullest exercise of professional academic competencies and responsibilities. Together academic freedom and tenure insure that faculty members can discharge their professional research and teaching obligations without fear of any sanction being applied to them. Academic tenure succeeds in its fundamental function if it can insure that tenured faculty members simply can not be summarily dismissed or otherwise sanctioned at will by their employing colleges and universities. Because of tenure, the college or university, within the context of satisfactory academic due process, first must show "adequate cause" for dismissal or for application of a lesser sanction. However "adequate cause" is defined, that definition must "be related, directly and substantially, to the fitness of faculty members in their *professional capacities* as teachers or researchers,"[21] and cannot properly include as a dismissal ground any exercise of any aspect of academic freedom or other rights of American citizens such as freedom of speech. Once these two requirements have been met, a tenured faculty member may be dismissed from academic employment or otherwise sanctioned, but not before.

C. Academic Tenure Primarily Affords Procedure Protections

With the exception of one rebuttable presumption which is substantive, academic tenure fundamentally provides only procedural due process protections and not any substantive rights, such as a right to lifetime employment. The professional job security that is provided by tenure derives from its procedural protections afforded its substantive rebuttable presumption (which presumption is strictly related to professional competence and to exercises of academic freedom, and is discussed below). Tenure's protection includes prohibitions against discriminatory reduction in salary or benefits,

---

[20] For discussion see the Presidential Address given at the 50th meeting of the AAUP on April 10, 1964, by F. Machlup, *In Defense to Academic Tenure*, 112 at pp. 120-21, AAUP Bulletin (Summer 1964). An analysis of Academic Freedom and the Nontenured Faculty Member is beyond the scope of this Study; however, for discussion of that subject see W. Van Alstyne, *Tenure: A Summary, Explanation and "Defense*," 328 at pp. 331-333, AAUP BULL. (Summer, 1971).

[21] AAUP's 1982 Recommended Institutional Regulations on Academic Freedom and Tenure, No 5(a), at p. 18a, ACADEME (Jan.-Feb. 1983). (Emphasis supplied.)

or other opportunities that are made generally available to faculty members, as well as against wrongful dismissal and unfair imposition of other lesser sanctions. In a fundamental sense, tenure's procedural requirement of due process only guarantees basic procedural fairness by the institution when dealing with tenured faculty members about quite important concerns, such as dismissal.

Due process is independent of the charge lodged against a faculty member. In dismissal cases where the charge is incontrovertibly genuine, serious and raises no question of academic freedom (for example, a charge that a faculty member repeatedly has accepted sexual favors in return for grades) the need remains for full procedural, academic due process in order to protect the individual and the institution from unreasonable risks of error and prejudice, and to do justice while resolving that serious charge. The felt needs to do justice and to base judgment on truth, thereby avoiding risks of error and prejudice are greater, and are more obvious, when the charge against a faculty member is, itself, not genuine but a subterfuge designed to mask an administration's retaliation for a faculty member's exercise of academic freedom or an exercise of a citizen's constitutional rights, such as the right to free speech. The fundamental justifications of defeasible job security afforded by fair procedural protection — due process protecting against an unjust forfeiture of a tenured professor's livelihood — is a simple concept readily understood.

D. Tenure's Rebuttable Presumption of Professional Competence

Properly viewed, tenure means only that after a person has been continuously employed by an institution of higher learning beyond a specified and lengthy period of probationary service that person cannot be summarily dismissed at will by a college or university. First the institution must demonstrate *adequate cause* and afford fully fair *due process* procedures. The conferral of tenure on a faculty member means that an American college or university has, or should have, carefully and rigorously scrutinized the professional competence and responsibility of that faculty member during a probationary period of employment as long as six years, and that after such ample opportunity to make a fully informed judgment on evidence of the candidate's professional competence and responsibility, the institution has rendered a favorable judgment conferring tenure which simultaneously established a rebuttable substantive presumption of that person's professional competence and responsibility. That rebuttable presumption of professional competence and responsibility is a *substantive* presumption, which can be removed only if the institution shows *adequate cause* for removal, at a hearing affording *sufficient procedural due process*.

The rebuttable substantive presumption of a faculty member's professional competence and responsibility created by the grant of tenure remains only that —a rebuttable substantive presumption of professional excellence. It can be rebutted precisely to the extent that the college or university can show that the tenured faculty member in question has fallen professionally short, or has otherwise misconducted himself or herself, in ways that directly, negatively and drastically affect his or her professional competence and responsibility. If proof is sufficient, the presumption of professional competence and responsibility is lost and the faculty member can be dismissed.

The purpose of a tenure hearing is justly and thoroughly to determine, preferably by a group of the charged faculty member's faculty peers, three facts regarding the rebuttable substantive presumption of professional competence and responsibility, in the context of a fully-fair due process hearing:[22]

1. that the stated cause is the authentic cause for dismissal, rather than a pretense or a makeweight for considerations invading academic freedom or ordinary personal civil liberties of the individual;
2. that the stated cause exists in fact;
3. that the degree of demonstrated professional irresponsibility warrants outright termination of the individual's appointment rather than some lesser sanction, even after taking into account the balance of his entire service and the personal consequences of dismissal.

E. "Adequate Cause" For Dismissal

"Adequate cause" for dismissal is, obviously, a very important element of any tenure system, and its proper and precise definition is of crucial importance. However, a welter of definitions exist in American higher education. Section 5(a) of the American Association of University Professors *1982 Recommended Institutional Regulations on Academic Freedom and Tenure* properly reflects the interdependence of tenure and academic freedom and provides that all definitions of adequate cause and their applications should have the following relational characteristics:[23]

---

[22] For further discussion see, W. Van Alstyne, *Tenure: A Summary Explanation and "Defense,"* p. 328, AAUP BULL. (Summer, 1971), stating the three inquiries quoted above and suggesting other ideas incorporated herein.

[23] ACADEME, 15a at p. 18a, (Jan.-Feb. 1983).

> Adequate cause for a dismissal will be related, directly and substantially, to the fitness of faculty members in their professional capacities as teachers or researchers. Dismissal will not be used to restrain faculty members in their exercise of academic freedom or other rights of American citizens.

The particular standards of "adequate cause" to which faculty members at any particular institution are accountable are themselves subject to definition by that institution, and should be defined specifically and set forth in the institution's published rules and regulations of general applicability. Generally, they are acceptable so long as an institution's defining rules of "adequate cause" are specified, published in advance, and formulated in specific language that is related, directly and substantially, to the fitness of faculty members in their professional capacities as teachers or researchers, and further, they must not violate academic freedom or the ordinary rights of American citizens either in their textual statement or when applied.

There are in America about 3,500 colleges and universities of widely varying size, quality and complexity. Given the traditional diversity of institutional objectives and commitments of American colleges and universities — a diversity to be encouraged rather than reduced — institutions should, within the requirements quoted above, have the responsibility for formulating their own definitions of "adequate cause" for dismissal that are unique to their missions. For example, if appropriate to its educational mission, "adequate cause" could be defined by a college or university to permit dismissal of a tenured faculty member for failure to meet an institution's published rule requiring a precisely stated and measurable amount of a specific type of teaching performance or scholarly research productivity from each faculty member per some fixed time period.

However, a 1971 study revealed that of eighty colleges and universities surveyed, roughly only one-half of them provided specific grounds for dismissal of tenured faculty members beyond the terms "adequate cause" or merely "cause." The institutions that did specify grounds collectively supplied some twenty-five different grounds for dismissing tenured faculty members.[24] After exhaustively reviewing this area, the 1973 Commission on Academic Tenure in Higher Education reluctantly repeated a key sentence from the *AAC-AAUP 1958 Statement On Procedural Standards In Faculty Dismissal Proceedings* stating that "one persistent source of diffi-

---

[24] B. Shaw, ACADEMIC TENURE IN AMERICAN HIGHER EDUCATION, at pp. 62-65 (1971).

culty is the definition of adequate cause for the dismissal of a faculty member," and then recommended as follows:[25]

> The commission believes that "adequate cause" in faculty dismissal proceedings should be restricted to (a) demonstrated incompetency or dishonesty, (b) substantial and manifest neglect of duty, and (c) personal conduct which substantially impairs the individual's fulfillment of his institutional responsibilities. The burden of proof in establishing cause for dismissal rests upon the institution.

A conclusion emerging from this discussion of "adequate cause" for dismissal is that neither the AAUP recommendation set forth above, identifying the common relational characteristics that all definitions of "adequate cause" should share, nor the recommendations on "adequate cause" by an enlightened Keast Commission, nor the actual and varied definitions of "adequate cause" promulgated by individual institutions of higher learning, involve the claim that the institution of academic tenure in any way necessarily insulates a faculty member from rendering a fair and reasonable accounting to the institution relying on that faculty member for the appropriate discharge of his or her professional responsibilities and for the reasonable maintenance of his or her professional competence.

F. Academic Tenure And Sanctions Short Of Dismissal

The concept of tenure, properly understood, admits sanctions short of dismissal to be applied to tenured faculty members in appropriate circumstances. Every college or university may adopt a careful statement of specifically identified sanctions short of dismissal that might be applied to tenured faculty members in cases of demonstrated professional misconduct or irresponsibility. Moreover, their accompanying due-process procedures that will govern the requirements for the complaint, hearing, faculty composition of the hearing committee and judgment may be less in the clearly less severe sanction cases, such as a reprimand, than those required for dismissal or in severe sanction cases. The less severe sanctions, such as reprimands, which give rise to lesser cases need not be treated in exactly the same procedural manner as dismissal cases, "especially as this may mean on the one hand that just grievances may simply go unredressed because of the discouragement that the elaborateness of dismissal procedures imposes upon the aggrieved party and upon the institution, and as it may mean on the other

---

[25] W.R. Keast and J.W. Macy, Jr., FACULTY TENURE, pp. 73 and 75 (1973). This Study organizes its discussion of cause using the Commission's formulations.

hand that the institution is frankly encouraged to seek more devious and subliminal ways of disciplining its faculty."[26] In the event that sanctions more severe than a reprimand may be applied to a faculty member, it is necessary that the full array of due process available in a dismissal proceeding be afforded.

The following sanctions are among the lesser sanctions, short of dismissal, that the concept of tenure admits so long as they are applied in the context of appropriate due process, and only in cases of demonstrated professional misconduct or irresponsibility: (1) an unrecorded oral reprimand; (2) an unrecorded written reprimand; (3) a recorded reprimand placed in the faculty member's personnel file; (4) restitution (for example, payment for damage intentionally or grossly negligently done to institutional property or to that of other university personnel); (5) loss of prospective benefits for a stated period of time such as suspension of eligibility for "across-the-board" or "merit" salary increases or promotion; (6) a fine for malicious unprofessional conduct; (7) reduction in salary for a stated period; and (8) suspension from employment for a stated period, but without any other prejudice attached.

It would be appropriate for an institution's published rules and regulations to provide that all sanctions less severe than dismissal should be used only as corrective action, seeking constructively to correct the underlying transgression rather than to be punitive, and concentrating on the prevention of serious personnel problems from arising in the future. Seen from this perspective of "progressive discipline" with dismissal as the final sanction, the lesser sanctions approach constitutes part of a college's or university's follow-through method of discipline, seeking to ensure that professional infractions, misconduct or unacceptable performance are treated as serious but in as constructive a manner as possible that will eliminate, correct or resolve them by helping the faculty member change his or her conduct. A major purpose of this kind of approach is to prevent future grave acts of professional misconduct by giving the faculty member an early warning of the possible consequences that may lie ahead if he or she persists in unacceptable behavior. A collateral consequence is that most of the lesser sanctions also create a document placed in a faculty member's personnel record that later will be of considerable evidentiary importance if corrective measures fail and it becomes necessary to institute a dismissal hearing.

---

[26] AAUP BULL., at pp. 524-27 (December, 1971).

G.   Faculty Dismissals Not Directly Protected By Tenure

Not every dismissal of a tenured faculty member can result in a tenure hearing with its full panoply of tenure's procedural protections. From time to time, two circumstances occur in higher education in which tenure does not afford much protection at all, even to tenured professors of the highest excellence. These two circumstances show beyond doubt that the institution of tenure does *not* require an entire college or university to suffer hardship rather than individual members of its tenured faculty.

The first circumstance is program elimination (or reduction). If, a college or university properly concludes on educational grounds that it will reduce or eliminate an academic program, then tenure provides no tenured faculty member within the ill-fated program with any guarantee against becoming a casualty of institutional programmatic change, even though the faculty member may be of the highest excellence, unless he or she is (1)able and willing to retrain to new professional competence which (2) is needed in some other academic program having sufficient support to sustain that faculty member's employment within the college or university. Otherwise, a tenured faculty member's employment is simply terminated with the elimination of the program itself.[27]

---

[27]   In Browzin v. Catholic Univ., 527 F.2d 843 (D.C. Cir. 1975), the federal Court of Appeals ruled that the University's rules committed it to "an obligation to make every effort to find [Professor Browzin] another suitable position in the institution." Program reduction or elimination must be *bona fide*. In D'Andrea v. Adams, 626 F.2d 469 (1980), a tenured assistant professor at Troy State University, Dr. Nicholas D'Andrea, in November 1976 spoke to an examiner preparing legislative budget hearings for TSU about certain persons who allegedly made improper use of TSU funds. TSU was later given a "clean bill of health" by the committee. In January 1977, Dr. D'Andrea was told that (at a meeting attended only by administrators) a decision was made eliminating the geography program and his position from the University. He sought a position in another division, but to no avail. He was unemployed. However, before the beginning of fall semester, the University decided its previous decision was precipitious because geography was a necessary component for a degree in elementary education and because enrollment data showed a burgeoning interest in the subject. So, the University reinstituted geography as a minor study area, with D'Andrea re-employed to teach the courses. In the meantime, he had filed this lawsuit against President Adams, claiming that the program's elimination was a mere subterfuge and that he was dismissed in retaliation for exercising his right of free speech. A jury agreed, and its award was affirmed on appeal, along with an award of his attorney fees and expenses. *Compare* Brumbach v. Rensselaer, 510 N.Y.S. 2d 761 (1987), "the faculty voted not to continue the position of assistant professor/contract archeologist, but rather to pursue a new direction," at the end of a probationary faculty member's first three-year contract, who had received a salary increase and favorable faculty evaluations during each year she occupied the abandoned position. The University's rules stated, "if the result of the evaluation is satisfactory, it is normal for an assistant professor to be re-employed for a second three-year period." Thereafter, the University created a new replacement position, a part-time tenure-track position emphasizing computer archeology, for which the non-renewed faculty member did not apply, but sued, claiming the University rules were part of her contract and that the University breached. The court ruled that the "manner and method" which changed the program's direction "was not arbitrary or unreasonable"; that at the expiration of her three-year contract, the faculty member, in law, became an employee at will who could be terminated without the institution having to show "just and sufficient cause," and that therefore, the faculty member's law suit should be dismissed.

Financial exigency is a second circumstance showing that the institution of tenure does *not* require an entire institution of higher education to suffer hardship rather than individual members of its tenured faculty. If an authentic condition of financial stringency confronts a college or university and academic programs must be eliminated because of *bona fide* financial reasons, then decisions identifying the programs and their sequence for elimination must be made. So long as these decisions are made in a reasonable and non-arbitrary way, and a *bona fide* financial exigency actually exists,[28] then tenure does nothing at all to insulate from unemployment a faculty member who previously served with excellence and high distinction in a program that was eliminated because of financial exigency.[29] The tenured faculty member is simply terminated when the program in which he or she served is terminated.[30]

---

[28] *See* Pace v. Hymas, 726 P.2d 693 (Idaho 1986), for a State Supreme Court ruling that a dismissal for financial exigency was wrongful because "reasonable and persuasive" evidence "clearly shows that the [State University] did not satisfy the requirements for proving a financial exigency; [the University] did not demonstrate a 'bona fide, immanent financial crisis . . . which cannot be adequately alleviated by means other than a reduction in the employment force.'" *But compare* Milbauer v. Keppler, 644 F. Supp. 201 (D. Idaho 1986); AAUP v. Bloomfield College, 346 A.2d 615 (N.J. 1975); and *also see*, Krotkoff v. Goucher College, 585 F.2d 675 (4th Cir. 1978).

[29] The court in Graney v. University of Wis., 286 N.W.2d 138 (Wis. Ct. App. 1979), stated:
> A concept of tenure that permits dismissal based on financial exigency is consistent with the primary purpose of tenure. Tenure's "real concern is with arbitrary or retaliatory dismissals based on an administrator's or a trustee's distaste for the content of a professor's teaching or research, or even for positions taken completely outside the campus setting . . . . It is designed to foster our society's interest in the unfettered progress of research and learning by protecting the profession's freedom of inquiry and instruction." Dismissals based on financial exigency, unlike those for cause or disability, are impersonal; they are unrelated to the views of the dismissed teachers. A professor whose appointment is terminated because of financial exigency will not be replaced by another with more conventional views or better connections. Hence, *bona fide* dismissals based on financial exigency do not threaten the values protected by tenure.

[30] Non-tenured faculty may receive even less protection. One judge has ruled that uncooperativeness on the part of a non-tenured faculty member justifiably made that faculty member an appropriate target for non-renewal in a situation of financial exigency. Cherry v. Burnett, 444 F. Supp. 324, 333 (Maryland 1977): "Young, impatient and without much experience as a college instructor, plaintiff Dean had a number of disputes with Dean Dedmond and felt that she was not being treated properly. Because of her aggressive and uncooperative attitude, plaintiff Dean was a logical candidate for non-renewal when it became necessary for President Burnett to reduce the size of the Choppin faculty in the Spring of 1974."

III. THE LEGAL ASPECTS OF TENURE

A. Introduction

This section addresses the legal aspects of academic tenure, seeking to identify whether the law faithfully implements the concept of tenure by providing a legally flexible tool which readily permits the dismissal of tenured faculty members of demonstrated incompetence or dishonesty, or who substantially and manifestly neglect their duties, or whether tenure, because of its legal aspects, either does not permit such dismissals or permits them only at unwarrantedly high costs, and thereby so deleteriously impacts institutions of higher learning that they currently are significantly deterred, or precluded, from achieving their educational goals.

Beginning with an identification of the emerging constitutional protection afforded the concepts of academic freedom and tenure, the Study moves to a discussion of the degree of deference courts actually give to academic administrators in personnel matters when dealing with professional competencies (unless the case also involves the additional claim of a violation of a constitutional or other legal right by institutional authorities). Next appears a discussion of retaliatory dismissal of faculty members for exercising a legal right; these cases do involve the claim that institutional authorities have violated a constitutional or other legal right. This section is followed by a brief discussion of procedural "due process of law"; that is, of constitutionally required legal procedures. Thereafter, the next section focuses on dimensions of "adequate cause," as revealed by cases involving dismissal of a tenured faculty member on grounds of demonstrated incompetence or dishonesty, or substantial and manifest neglect of professional duty (including insubordination).

B. Constitutional Protection For The Concept Of Academic Freedom

Although it is not one of the rights expressly enumerated in the First Amendment, in 1959 the Supreme Court of the United States recognized the societal importance and the constitutional status of academic freedom, stating that when "academic teaching-freedom and its corollary learning — freedom, so essential to the well-being of the Nation, are claimed [in a case], this Court will always be on the alert against intrusion by Congress [and other branches of government] into this constitutionally protected domain."[31] Later in 1967, the Court further recognized that academic freedom lies at the very core of the First Amendment, and based its decision, in part, on the concept of academic freedom; however, it did not rule, and had no occasion to rule in the case, that all of the concept's dimensions are protected by the First Amendment. The Court left such possible rulings for future cases. It did, however, carefully acknowledge that:[32]

> Our Nation is deeply committed to safeguarding academic freedom, which is of transcendent value to all of us and not merely to the teachers concerned. That freedom is therefore a special concern of the First Amendment, which does not tolerate laws that cast a pall of orthodoxy over the classroom. "The vigilant protection of constitutional freedoms is nowhere more vital than in the community of American schools." . . . The classroom is peculiarly the "marketplace of ideas." The Nation's future depends upon leaders trained through wide exposure to that robust exchange of ideas which discovers truth "out of a multitude of tongues, [rather] than through any kind of authoritative selection." . . . In *Sweezy v. State of New Hampshire*, 354 U.S. 234, 250, 77 S.Ct. 1203, 1211, 1 L. Ed.2d 1311, we said:
>
>> "The essentiality of freedom in the community of American universities is almost self-evident. No one should underestimate the vital role in a democracy that is played by those who guide and train our youth. To impose any strait jacket upon the intellectual leaders in our colleges and

---

[31] Barenblatt v. United States, 360 U.S. 109, 112 (1959). *See also* Byrne, *Academic Freedom: A Special Concern Of The First Amendment*, 99 YALE L.J. 251 (1989); *Symposium On Academic Freedom*, 66 TEXAS L. REV. 1274 (1988); Yudof, *Three Faces Of Academic Freedom*, 32 LOY. L. REV. 831 (1987); Rabban, *Academic Freedom*, in 1 ENCYCLOPEDIA OF THE AMERICAN CONSTITUTION 12 (L. Levy, K. Karst & P. Mahoney eds. 1986); and Van Alstyne, *The Constitutional Rights Of Teachers And Professors*, 1970 DUKE LAW J. 841.

[32] Keyishian v. Board of Regents, 385 U.S. 589, 603 (1967) (the court ruled unconstitutional parts of New York's "subversive control" laws that were vague and overly broad, and impinged on academic freedom). "Academic freedom, though not a specifically enumerated constitutional right, long has been viewed as a special concern of the First Amendment," Regents v. Bakke, 438 U.S. 265, 312 (1978). Case law identifying the parameters of the protection afforded academic freedom have yet to be fully worked out on a case by case basis. But it is "clear that whatever constitutional protection is afforded by the First Amendment extends as readily to the scholar in the laboratory as to the teacher in the classroom." Dow Chemical Co. v. Allen, 672 F.2d 1262 (7th Cir. 1982). For general commentary on the law see, T. Emerson, *The System Of Freedom Of Expression* at p. 594 (1970) and Note, *Developments In the Law — Academic Freedom*, 81 HARV. L. REV. 1045 (1968), and references in notes 38 and 41.

universities would imperil the future of our Nation. No
field of education is so thoroughly comprehended by man
that new discoveries cannot yet be made. Particularly is
that true in the social sciences, where few, if any, principles
are accepted as absolutes. Scholarship cannot flourish in
an atmosphere of suspicion and distrust. Teachers and
students must always remain free to inquire, to study and to
evaluate, to gain new maturity and understanding; otherwise our civilization will stagnate and die."

Like other constitutional rights, a faculty member's right to academic
freedom is not absolute and on occasion, in the appropriate kind of case
where grave political, countervailing considerations are implicated, courts
will balance a faculty member's right to academic freedom against compet-
ing political interests. For example, in the *Barenblatt* case, *supra*, the
Supreme Court recognized academic freedom in 1959. But, it also upheld
Barenblatt's conviction for contempt of Congress because he refused to
answer a congressional investigating committee's questions about Communist Party membership — national security was believed to be at stake and
the investigation was not directed at controlling what was taught at the
university (although somewhat impinging on it) but at violent overthrow of
government.[33] Precedential case law "at the Supreme Court level suggests
that to prevail over academic freedom the [political] interests of government
that the Supreme Court balances must be strong and the extent of the
intrusion carefully limited."[34]

In other cases courts have balanced a claim of academic freedom against
legal procedures that are invasive but necessary to obtain evidence to prove
a case. For example, the Supreme Court recently ruled there is no qualified
privilege of academic freedom available to protect the materials created
during academic peer review of a probationary teacher up for tenure from
discovery by the EEOC in a Title VII investigation where the tenure-denied
faculty member has alleged that race, sex or national origin discrimination

---

[33] Barenblatt, 360 U.S. 109, 112, 129, 130 (1959).
[34] Dow Chemical Co. v. Allen, 672 F.2d 1262, 1275 (7th Cir. 1982), (relying *inter alia* on Sweezy
v. New Hampshire, 354 U.S. 234 (1957) and especially on Justice Frankfurter's concurrence (354
at p. 262): "[A]cademic inquiries . . . must be left as unfettered as possible. Political power [but not
inquiry by university colleagues where there are reasons to suspect incompetence, etc. which are
exigent and compelling] must abstain from intrusion into this activity of freedom, pursued in the
interest of wise government and the people's well-being, except for reasons that are exigent and
obviously compelling.")

occurred when the tenure decision was made.[35] There have been very few court cases that directly turn on claims of academic freedom, and fewer still that clearly present only a pure question of academic freedom.

C. Constitutional Protection of Tenure as a "Property" Interest

In 1972, the Supreme Court completed its recognition of constitutional protection for the interrelated concepts of academic freedom and tenure by ruling that a tenured faculty member at a *public* institution, because of the existence of a *de facto* or *de jure* tenure system, had a constitutionally protected property interest under the Fourteenth Amendment which could not be taken away by summarily dismissing a tenured faculty member. Like its decisions in the academic freedom area, the Court did not rule, nor did it have occasion to rule, that all of the dimensions of the concept of tenure are protected by the Fourteenth Amendment, leaving such possibility to be resolved in the future on a case-by-case basis. One should be clear that the Court did not rule that a state college or university must create a tenure system if it doesn't otherwise have one because of the Fourteenth Amendment. But rather, if a public institution has a tenure system, in law or fact, then, the Court ruled, tenured faculty members also had a "property" interest protected by the Fourteenth Amendment's command that government "shall not deprive any person of . . . property without due process of law." Before dismissing a tenured faculty member, the employing state college or university first must show adequate cause at a hearing held within the framework of satisfactorily fair due-process procedures:[36]

---

[35] University of Pa. v. EEOC, 110 S. Ct. 577 (1990), and *see*, Finkin, *On "Institutional" Academic Freedom*, 61 TEXAS L. REV. 817 (1983), *also compare*, Dixon v. Rutgers, 541 A.2d 1046 (N.J. 1988) (agreeing that no qualified academic freedom privilege exists, but the New Jersey court went on to craft a set of rules limiting the availability of peer review materials on discovery). For commentary, *see*, Note, University of Pa. v. EEOC and Dixon v. Rutgers: *Two Supreme Courts Speak On The Academic Freedom Privilege*, 42 RUTGERS L. REV. 1089 (1990).

[36] Perry v. Sindermann, 408 U.S. 593, 601 (1972), *but compare*, Board of Regents v. Roth, 408 U.S. 564 (1972) (holding that a non-tenured, probationary faculty member had no protectable property interest at the expiration of the employment contract). For discussion *see*, W. Kaplin, THE LAW OF HIGHER EDUCATION, 168-172 (1985).

The Fourteenth Amendment applies only to state colleges and universities, and the Perry case directly applies only there. On the other hand, unless prevented by some convincing reason, courts almost always will incorporate an institution's tenure rules and regulations into the contract of employment of faculty members in private (and public) institutions, even where the contracts are silent and do not provide for such incorporation. Adamian v. Jacobsen, 523 F.2d 929, 932-32 (9th Cir. 1975); Brady v. Trustees of Neb. State Colleges, 242 N.W. 2d 616 (Neb. 1976), and *see*, Brown, *Tenure Rights In Contractual and Constitutional Context*, 6 J. OF LAW & ED. 279, 282-84 (1977). Moreover, courts further will assume, in appropriate circumstances, that faculty members' contracts also include the AAC-AAUP 1940 Statement Of Principles On Academic Freedom And Tenure, and additional AAUP guidelines because the Statement and the guidelines represent the standards of

> We have made clear . . . that "property" interests subject to
> procedural due process protection are not limited by a few
> rigid, technical forms. Rather, "property" denotes a broad
> range of interests that are secured by "existing rules or
> understandings." . . . A person's interest in a benefit is a
> "property" interest for due process purposes if there are
> such rules or mutually explicit understandings that support
> his claim of entitlement to the benefit and that he may
> invoke at a hearing. . . . A written contract with an explicit
> tenure provision clearly is evidence of a formal under-
> standing that supports a teacher's claim to continued em-
> ployment unless sufficient "cause" is shown.

Finally, in the 1985 decision, *Cleveland Board of Education v. Loudermill*[37] the Supreme Court further protected tenure with another requirement of procedural due process. It ruled that persons having a property interest in their employment, such as civil service employees or tenured faculty members employed at state colleges and universities, cannot be summarily removed from their employment, even temporarily, and thereby be deprived of their property interests even if a procedurally satisfactory full, due-process hearing would necessarily ensue later, but instead, the Fourteenth Amendment generally requires that there must first be an informal pre-deprivation hearing before a person can be even tempo- rarily deprived of his or her property interest in tenure. *Loudermill's* required

---

professional academic practice in this country; *see e.g.,* Hill v. Talladega College, 502 So. 2d 735, 737 (Ala. 1987), or courts may interpret a faculty member's employment contract against the backdrop of the AAC-AAUP's 1940 Statement Of Principles On Academic Freedom And Tenure, to imply the power to terminate appointments due to financial exigency because, the Statement is the "most widely-accepted academic definition of tenure." Krotkoff v. Goucher College, 585 F.2d 675 (4th Cir. 1978), *also see* the following cases relying on AAUP documents: Bason v. American Univ., 414 A.2d 522, 525 (D.C. 1980); Pride v. Howard Univ., 384 A.2d 31, 35 (D.C. 1978); Browzin v. Catholic Univ., 527 F.2d 843, 845-46 (D.C. Cir. 1975); Greene v. Howard Univ., 134 U.S. App. D.C. 81, 88, 412 F.2d 1128, 1135 (1969), and McConnell v. Howard Univ., *supra.* Thus, tenured faculty members at private institutions of higher learning must rely upon the tenure provisions in their contracts of employment for legal protection suing, if necessary, for breach of contract, rather than for deprivation of a "property" interest as in Perry, *supra. See e.g.,* McConnell v. Howard Univ., 818 F.2d 58 (D.C. Cir. 1987). Because of the commonness of the interests involved, there is frequently a considerable degree of overlap of the legal interpretation in the two situations, but it is by no means always identical.

[37] Cleveland Bd. of Educ. v. Loudermill, 470 U.S. 532, 542 and 545-46 (1985):
An essential principle of due process is that a deprivation of life, liberty, or property, "be preceded by notice and opportunity for hearing appropriate to the nature of the case." We have described "the root requirement" of the Due Process Clause as being "that an individual be given an opportunity for a hearing *before* he is deprived of any significant property interest." . . . This principle requires "some kind of a hearing" prior to the discharge of an employee who has a constitutionally protected property interest in his employment.

hearing need not be elaborate, neither fully formal nor completely comprehensive, so long as a fully complete hearing necessarily will follow soon after the informal pre-deprivation hearing. The Supreme Court ruled only that three conditions must be satisfied prior to the fully complete hearing on termination:[38]

> The essential requirements of due process . . . are notice and an opportunity to respond. The opportunity to present reasons, either in person or in writing, why proposed action should not be taken is a fundamental due process requirement. "The tenured public employee is entitled to oral or written notice of the charges against him, an explanation of the employer's evidence, and an opportunity to present his side of the story." . . . To require more than this prior to termination would intrude to an unwarranted extent on the government's interest in quickly removing an unsatisfactory employee. . . . We conclude that all the process that is due is provided by a pretermination opportunity to respond, coupled with post-termination administrative procedures as provided by the Ohio statute.

The purpose of *Loudermill's* informal hearing is to provide a check against mistaken decisions — essentially a determination of whether there are reasonable grounds to believe that the charges against the public employee are supported and may likely be true. However, one should be very clear that before the Fourteenth Amendment provides any protection whatsoever, the claimed interest must, itself, qualify as a "property interest" and not all interests that have been claimed by faculty members in public institutions have qualified.[39]

---

[38] *Id.*

[39] In Maples v. Martin, 858 F.2d 1546, 1550 (11th Cir. 1988), the court ruled that a transfer of a tenured professor from the Department of Mechanical Engineering at Auburn University to another engineering department at Auburn did not raise a tenure question because "transfers and reassignments have generally not been held to implicate a property interest." *See also*, Garvie v. Jackson, 845 F.2d 647, 651 (6th Cir. 1988) (no property interest at issue when Department Head is reassigned to regular teaching duties); Childers v. Independent Sch. Dist., 676 F.2d 1338, 1341 (10th Cir. 1982) (tenured teacher has a property interest in continued employment but not in particular assignment), and Kelleher v. Flawn, 761 F.2d 1079, 1087 (5th Cir. 1985) (reappointment of non-tenured faculty member with concurrent reduction of teaching duties does not deprive faculty member of property interest).

D. Judicial Deference to Institutional Decisions Dismissing Tenured Faculty Members on Grounds of Incompetency, Dishonesty or Neglect of Duty

All American courts, whether federal or state, afford a considerably large amount of deference to personnel decisions made by institutions of higher education, including decisions involving dismissals of tenured faculty members, especially in cases that do not also involve any additional claims of violations of constitutional rights such as academic freedom or free speech, or claims of violations of other constitutional or legal rights such as rights to due-process procedures. In the simplest cases of professional competency and responsibility the only question is whether the institution's decision afforded the tenured faculty member *substantive* (not procedural) due process of law. Courts are particularly loathe to find violations of "substantive" due process of law and to substitute their decisions for final dismissal decisions made by college or university officials whenever the sole question in a dismissal case is one of professional competence or responsibility, and especially so when institutional decisions solely involve questions concerning what constitutes adequate teaching or research:[40]

> [T]he administration of the internal affairs of a college and especially the determination of professional competency is a matter peculiarly within the discretion of a college administration. . . . Due process should not be employed to insure that the exercise of discretion is "wise" but only that it is not unreasonable, arbitrary or capricious.

Indeed, courts are particularly deferential to governing boards with respect to all personnel decisions generally:[41]

> The management of the university is primarily the responsibility of those equipped with the special skills and sensitivities necessary for so delicate a task. One of the most sensitive functions of the university administration is the appointment, promotion, and retention of the faculty. It is for this reason that the courts, and administrative agencies as well, should "only rarely assume academic oversight,

---

[40] Chung v. Park, 514 F.2d 382, 387 (3d. Cir. 1975), *cert. denied,* 423 U.S. 948 (1975) (quoted approvingly in Johnson v. Lincoln Univ., 776 F.2d 443, 455 (3d Cir. 1985)).

[41] New York Inst. of Technology v. State Div. of Human Rights, 353 N.E.2d 598 (1976), (quoting Matter of Pace College v. Committee on Human Rights of N.Y., 339 N.E.2d 880 (1975)). The court's words echo those of the U.S. Supreme Court uttered in a case involving the K-12 context, but seem equally applicable to higher education as well: "It is not the role of the federal courts to set aside decisions of school administrators which the court may view as lacking a basis in wisdom or compassion." Wood v. Strickland, 420 U.S. 308, 326 (1975).

except with the greatest caution and restraint, in such
sensitive areas as faculty appointment, promotion, and
tenure, especially in institutions of higher learning."

In dismissal cases coming to courts from *public* colleges and universities
involving no consideration other than that of substantive professional
competence and responsibility (or manifest and substantial neglect of professional duty), the only issue for courts usually is whether the public institution
afforded the tenured faculty member substantive "due process of law" which
translates into the further question: Was the decision to dismiss reasonably
based on "substantial evidence" or was it "clearly erroneous"? If based on
"substantial evidence," that is the end of the case; if not and the terminating
decision was against the manifest weight of the evidence, courts will reverse
the decision labelling it "arbitrary and capricious" or "irrational." "'Substantial evidence' means evidence 'which possesses relevance and substance and
which furnishes a substantial basis of fact from which the issue can reasonably be resolved.'"[42] In other words, the question for the court is whether the
final decision of the public institution's governing board is clearly erroneous?[43] This rule does not require courts to judge the weight of the evidence
against a faculty member, mulling the evidence pro and con, and then to
determine whether the governing Board's decision to terminate a tenured
faculty member, in the judgment of the court, is supported either by clear and
convincing evidence or by a preponderance of the evidence. Unless some
law prescribes a different standard, the rule requires only that the final
terminating decision of a public institution not be clearly erroneous; that is,
it must be supported by "substantial evidence." As one federal court
expressed it:[44]

[The tenured faculty member, who was dismissed on the
ground of demonstrated incompetence] initially contends
that he was not accorded substantive due process, that is, he
asserts that there is not substantial evidence supporting the

---

[42] Haddock v. Board of Educ., 661 P.2d 368, 372 (Kan. 1983) (quoting Kelly v. Kansas City
Community College, 648 P.2d 225 (Kan. 1982)).

[43] "A [governing board] decision is clearly erroneous if, although there may be evidence to
support a finding, the reviewing court is left with the definite and firm conviction that a mistake has
been committed." Sinnott v. Skagit Valley College, 746 P.2d 1213 (Wash. Ct. App. 1987). "An
arbitrary and capricious act is one that is willful and unreasonable and done without [reference] to
the facts and circumstances of the case; an act without some basis which would lead a reasonable and
honest person to the same conclusion." Riggin v. Board of Trustees of Ball State Univ., 489 N.E.2d
616, 625 (Ind. Ct. App. 1986).

[44] King v. University of Minn., 774 F.2d 224, 227 (8th Cir. 1985). (This case illustrates proper
procedures; that is, "how to do it right." George King was a black, tenured full professor in the Liberal
Arts College's Department of Afro-American Studies. After a departmental vote of 9 to 2 to remove
King "from the Department because of his long history of disservice," and after receiving the
dismissal charges, King, represented by counsel throughout, "was allowed substantial documentary
discovery" and took depositions of the departmental chair and the current and former college deans,

decision of the University [of Minnesota] to terminate him for cause. It is, of course, not for the District Court or for this Court to determine *de novo* whether we would terminate [him] based on the evidence presented during the hearings afforded [the faculty member] by the University . . . . Rather, it was [the faculty member's] burden in this case to prove in the District Court that he was dismissed without being afforded . . . due process or that he was dismissed for a constitutionally impermissible reason. [He failed to do so.]

A state supreme court has stated the substantial evidence rule a bit more pointedly, identifying a three-pronged standard, and further noted that court review on appeal from final decisions of public institutions of higher education terminating tenured faculty members "is very limited":[45]

---

and after the parties had a pre-hearing conference after which the issues were identified and during which witness and exhibit lists were exchanged, a full, academic due process hearing was held wherein his lawyer presented evidence on King's behalf, cross-examined opposing witnesses and made oral and written arguments to the tenure hearing panel composed of King's academic peers. The panel recommended King's termination on the tenure code ground of "cause [that] seriously interferes with the person's capacity competently to perform his duties, or seriously interferes with his usefulness to the university." The verbatim transcript of the record revealed a history of "complaints about King's performance by students, colleagues, and by successive [Departmental] chairmen . . . concern[ing] poor teaching performance, excessive unexcused absences from class, absence from faculty meetings, low enrollment in his classes, undocumented research, and other matters." The governing board approved the Tenure Committee's recommendation, and King sued, but lost his case in the federal court where he claimed, but failed to prove: (1) that no substantial evidence supported the University's decision to terminate him for cause, contrary to the due process of law requirement; (2) that he was not accorded sufficient procedural due process of law, and (3) that he was discriminated against on racial grounds).

45   Kelly v. Kansas City Community College, 648 P.2d 225, 22 (Kan. 1982). (In one sense of the standard, this case raises issues which perhaps can be seen as falling within a charge broadly claiming the faculty members with manifest and substantial neglect of professional duties. The actual charges were (1) conduct detrimental to the nursing program, and (2) inability to cooperate and maintain harmony among the staff. Problems "between the nursing director and two [dismissed, tenured nursing] instructors affected the morale of the whole department," centering, at least in part, around a struggle for control over the direction of the nursing program. Faculty meetings were "tense" and "uneasy," and the nursing director testified there was "constant sniping" in nursing staff meetings. After receiving permission, a student decided not to take an exam early because it would cause problems between the nursing director and one of the instructors. The director later resigned in an attempt to solve the problems, but the new director testified that "complaints of not being able to work with [the two instructors] increased after she took over." Finally, members of a site-visiting, accrediting agency recommended group therapy-type processes be instituted for the faculty as a whole to help the faculty to find ways to work together. Whereupon, the new director recommended termination of the two tenured instructors. A hearing committee found "the Board had not sustained its burden of proof" on the two charges against the two tenured faculty members, and by a two-to-one vote the committee recommended that the two nursing instructor not be dismissed but be renewed for the next school year. The Board of Trustees rejected the committee's recommendation, and dismissed the two tenured instructors who appealed to state courts. A Kansas District Court and then Kansas' Supreme Court upheld their dismissal, applying the "substantial evidence" rule to the "final" decision of the educational institution; that of the governing board.)

> A district court may not, on appeal, substitute its judgment
> for that of an administrative tribunal, but is restricted to
> considering [1] whether, as a matter of law, the tribunal
> acted fraudulently, arbitrarily or capriciously [or in viola-
> tion of constitutional right], [2] whether the administrative
> order [of dismissal] is substantially supported by evidence,
> and [3] whether the tribunal's action was within the scope
> of its authority.

The reason for this deferential standard of judicial review of institutional decisionmaking is that a public educational institution is generally treated by law as though it is another governmental administrative agency. A tenure plan promulgated by the governing board of a *public* college or university — an administrative agency — is generally considered a form of sublegislation having the force of law; i.e., administrative law, which, in turn, is thereafter administered by administrative professionals and expert administrative managers of the agency. The officials of public educational institutions are officers of the administrative agency who are legally presumed by courts to have expertise in matters of academic affairs, including the expertise necessary to judge the professional competence and responsibility of tenured faculty members.[46] Academic disciplines and faculty members are quite unique in their professional dimensions, which are subjects on which courts are ill-equipped to pass judgment. In addition to considerations of expertise, generally lacking in courts, officials of administrative agencies generally are legally presumed to have obeyed the law and to have made decisions in a legally reasonable way whenever they make decisions that come within the scope of their delegated discretion. Thus, courts hold final administrative decisions to be *prima facie* true and correct on administrative review. Fact finding and decision by academic administrative agencies "when reached by correct procedures and supported by substantial evidence, are entitled to great weight, and the court should never lightly substitute its judgment for that of the board."[47] This judicial attitude has special "bite" when courts are asked to review final institutional decisions dismissing tenured faculty members solely due to a failure of professional competence and responsibility.

---

[46] "The court may not substitute its own opinions for that of the Board of Trustees, but must give deference to its expertise"; a "court will not interfere with the acts of an administrative agency which are within the agency's allowable scope of responsible discretion unless it found that the adminis-trative act was arbitrary, capricious, an abuse of discretion or unsupported by substantial evidence"; "the burden of proving that the administrative action was arbitrary or capricious falls on the party seeking to vacate the administrative order." Riggin v. Board of Trustees of Ball State Univ., 489 N.E.2d 616, 625 (Ind. Ct. App. 1986).

[47] Duke v. North Tex. State Univ., 469 F.2d 829, 859 (5th Cir. 1972), *and also see* Saunders v. Reorganized Sch. Dist., 520 S.W.2d 29, 35 (Mo. 1975).

Tenured faculty members attacking final administrative agency decisions dismissing them solely for lacking professional competence, honesty, or manifest and substantial neglect of duty do not receive a new trial, *de novo*, in the court. Instead they receive only court review of the record previously made by the public administrative agency prior to its decision (thus, the records made at the Tenure Hearing and before the Board are crucial to both sides), and when in court tenured faculty members must overcome the presumptions of legality enjoyed by decisions of administrative agency officers. Dismissed tenured faculty members must satisfactorily carry the burden of proving that the final decision of the administrative agency — that of the governing board — was legally wrong; that is, unreasonable under all the circumstances. This means the faculty member must prove the administrative board's decision to be "arbitrary and capricious" or "irrational" and when attempting to do so, faculty members are limited to appealing the evidence made part of the record during the earlier administrative agency's hearing.[48] That is a difficult burden to carry because the faculty member must prove that the terminating decision was against the manifest weight of the evidence.

Obviously, the state administrative agency model does not apply to *private* institutions of higher education. They do not receive delegations of law-making power from state legislatures or state constitutions. Their internal private rules and regulations on tenure, although a form of locally private sublegislation, do not have the force of public administrative law. In a private institution, any right to tenure is a contractual matter, rather than a matter of state administrative or statutory law or a federal constitutional law. A suit for breach of contract against a private institution for wrongful dismissal raises a contractual question, not the administrative law question whether an administrative agency official acted reasonably within his or her scope of decisionmaking. Courts are well equipped with expertise to interpret contracts of employment (just as they are well equipped to interpret administrative law) and to determine whether breach of contract has occurred.

The faculty member's employment contract almost always expressly will, or will be interpreted to, include the private institution's rules and regulations governing its tenure system.[49] If the contract calls for, and if the faculty member charged with demonstrated professional incompetence receives, an initial tenure hearing in the context of full academic due-process before a tribunal composed of his or her faculty peers, and if that tribunal decides against the faculty member, and its decision is later affirmed by the

---

[48] "A court may not reweigh the evidence or determine the credibility of witnesses." Riggin v. Board of Trustees of Ball State Univ., 489 N.E.2d 616, 625 (1986).

[49] *See* note 45, *supra*.

institution's governing board, then when courts consider the only real question presented by the case — whether the faculty member is professionally competent or incompetent — the role of the courts in such breach-of-contract cases is quite conventional.[50] The court most likely would judge only whether the faculty member had received the contractually-required tenure hearing and whether the decisions made by the Tenure Committee and the Board of Trustees can be judged to have been made in good faith in accordance with the contractually-required standard of clear and convincing evidentiary proof of professional incompetency or irresponsibility (or by whatever other standard might be required by the institution's tenure code) which is all that the tenured faculty member's contract requires. The burden the plaintiff, i.e. the tenured faculty member, must carry in the court is one of convincing the court that although he or she was judged to lack professional competence by the Tenure Committee and by the institution's governing board, the contract's procedural requirements really were not observed by the institution, or no tribunal could have applied the clear and convincing (or other required) standard to the evidence and in good faith reasonably conclude that the faculty member was incompetent, and that therefore, the tenured faculty member's dismissal was contrary to his or her employment contract.[51]

---

[50] After noting approvingly that Clark Byse and Louis Joughin had written thoughtfully about the role of courts when reviewing tenured faculty dismissals, and after quoting them as follows:

The role of the courts in reviewing dismissal determinations by institutions which have sound, written tenure plans should be quite conventional and relatively simple. It would be the court's responsibility to determine whether the requirements of the plan had been complied with. Was there failure to follow the stated procedure? Were the facts proved by a preponderance of the evidence? Did the proved facts constitute disqualifying conduct within the meaning of the plan?

(Byse & Joughin, *Tenure in American Higher Education*, reprinted in ACADEMIC FREEDOM AND TENURE at pp. 210, 214 (L. Joughin ed. 1969), the United States Court of Appeal for the District of Columbia stated that it could "find no reason not to do here what courts traditionally do in adjudicating breach of contract claims [by tenured faculty members in private institutions]: interpret the terms of the contract and determine whether the contract has been breached." McConnell v. Howard Univ., 818 F.2d 58, 70 (D.C. Cir. 1987).

[51] To the McConnell court, *supra*, "this means that a court must make a *de novo* determination of the facts and of the contract." McConnell v. Howard Univ., 818 F.2d 58, 70, n.4 (1987). But everything depends upon the requirements of each uniquely specific contract. In a non-academic context, the court stated that the contract's "meaning intended by the drafter, the employer, is controlling and there is no reason to infer that the employer intended to surrender its power to determine whether facts constituting cause for termination exist." Simpson v. Western Graphics Corp., 643 P.2d 1276, 1279 (1982). *Compare also* Clasby v. University of Miami, 356 So. 2d 915, 919 (1978) (". . . when examining a decision by a private university to deny tenure to a faculty member, this Court's scope of review is limited to a determination of whether there is substantial evidence in the record to support the decision of the university's governing body . . . . This Court is not to conduct a review *de novo* of the tenure decision. . . . To do so would require this Court to judge Plaintiff's qualifications and to substitute its judgment for the judgment of the Trustees. This would be contrary to that clause in the contract which states that 'nothing contained herein is to be construed as binding the Trustees of the University to vote in favor of tenure' and contrary to the controlling rule of law in this country." Query: Does such a contract clause also require the same kind of court review of the dismissal of a tenured faculty member?).

The "clear and convincing evidence" standard is more stringent than the "substantial evidence" rule that applies to court review of tenure dismissal decisions made by public institutions. It may appear that because of the way in which some contracts are worded, some tenured faculty members in a private institution may receive more court protection than a colleague in a public institution. But, in the case of dismissals of tenured faculty members, the public institution's Tenure Committee that initially decides the question of professional competence, just as its counterpart in a private institution, will apply the "clear and convincing evidence" standard (unless its tenure plan specifically calls for a different standard) and so should the public institution's Board of Regents or its President when the tenure committee's decision is appealed. Thus, to this point the same standard for judging the evidence is used in private and public institutions. Courts know this parallel history. But, the fact remains that courts are obliged to apply the less stringent "substantial evidence" rule to dismissal cases that come to them on administrative appeal from public institutions. Depending upon the requirements of the specific contract, a court may ask whether the stricter contractually-provided rule ("clear and convincing evidence") was applied in reasonably good faith to cases coming to them from private institutions on claims of breach-of-contract.[52]

However, the seeming advantage of being tenured in a private college or university may prove illusory because many courts are reluctant to decree specific performance of a personal service contract. Consequently, a court order of reinstatement will not generally favor a tenured faculty member in a private institution who has been dismissed, and has proved that his employment contract was breached. Money damages for the breach of contract will be the usual remedy. (Of course, the parties may voluntarily agree to reinstatement.) On the other hand, courts readily order reinstatement when public institutions fail to follow their tenure plans which are law, to the detriment of the faculty member.[53] Perhaps it is this fatal discrepancy that led C. Byse and L. Joughin to observe that "continuity of employment

---

52 *See* the cases in the preceding note.

53 In Endress v. Brookdale Community College, 364 A.2d 1080, 1091 (N.J. 1976), the court formulated this well-accepted rule as follows:

It is settled law, of course, as the trial judge here readily acknowledged, that personal service contracts are generally not specifically enforceable affirmatively. . . . But . . . it [is] no longer open to question that a public agency may neither dismiss from employment nor withhold renewal of a contract from a nontenured public employee for a reason or reasons founded upon the exercise of a constitutional right [or lacking substantial evidence support] . . . . In such case, the remedy of specific performance is appropriate.

But compare, AAUP v. Bloomfield College, 346 A.2d 615 (N.J. 1975) (dismissed tenured faculty members reinstated because the reason for their dismissal was the Board's desire to abolish tenure—a contractual right of faculty members—and not the declared ground of financial exigency, which indicates that the institution wrongfully breached its contract).

extended by an institution with a long and honorable tradition of academic freedom and tenure will often be much more meaningful than an express legal obligation grudgingly assumed by a lesser institution."[54]

An important conclusion becomes eminently clear from the way in which courts review decisions to dismiss where the sole issue is professional competency and responsibility. Court review of the legal aspects of tenure presents no legal impediment to the dismissal of tenured faculty members who have been properly demonstrated to lack substantive professional competence and responsibility.

E. Judicial Review of Institutional Decisions Dismissing Tenured Faculty Members Alleging Retaliation for Exercise of Academic Freedom or a Constitutional Right

The immediate preceding section demonstrates that the legal aspects of the concept of tenure constitute no significant substantive barrier to procedurally correct dismissals of professionally incompetent tenured faculty members in cases where professional competency or neglect of duty is the sole issue. Courts give large amounts of deference to substantive decisions of academic administrators and governing boards in personnel matters so long as they follow sound procedures. Courts are loathe to become involved: (1) in substantive disputes concerning the proper *substantive content* of professional standards and criteria such as whether a "lack of professional competence and responsibility in research and teaching" is too vague, subjective and amorphous,[55] or whether such a standard ought to serve as a legally adequate ground for dismissal of a tenured faculty member; and (2) in *substantive* disputes involving the question whether a faculty member actually meets the standard's *substantive* professional requirements of competence and responsibility.

Courts are considerably more willing to review faculty claims of deprivation of *rights*, whether *substantive* or *procedural* rights; for example, a claim that the tenured faculty member was dismissed by the institution without following proper procedures, or the faculty member was dismissed in retaliation for the exercise of a substantive constitutional right, such as freedom of speech or press (publication), rights held in common by all

---

[54] C. Byse and L. Joughin, TENURE IN AMERICAN HIGHER EDUCATION p. 75 (1959).

[55] Because of the vague and overly broad ways in which "cause" or "adequate cause" are stated in tenure codes, courts are timidly beginning to approach this area, as set forth below in text at note 111, *infra*.

American citizens.[56] The daily fare of courts consists in identifying whether a claimed legal right, substantive or procedural, actually exists in the context of a case before them, and if so, to protect it.

Retaliation cases present two claims: one of retaliation made by the faculty member and the other claim made by the governing board, usually that the tenured faculty member was really dismissed because of "insubordination" or "professional incompetence," or "uncooperativeness," or "neglect of duty," or even "encouraging immoral behavior." The key question in such cases is whether the governing board's ground is only a subterfuge because the faculty member exercised a constitutional right? This section of this Study will focus on retaliation cases involving a claim that the tenured faculty member's retaliatory discharge was based on his or her exercise of a *substantive* legal right. The next section will focus on claims of deprivation of *procedural* rights, but in a non-retaliatory context.

Even in cases that appear clear to any disinterested observer, courts have not always protected the exercise of *substantive* constitutional rights against retaliation. In 1960, Dr. Koch, a probationary biology professor at the University of Illinois, was successfully serving his fifth year of a six-year contract. He wrote a letter published in the school newspaper asserting that premarital sexual intercourse among college students is not, by itself, immoral or improper. A probationary, non-tenured faculty member at a public institution has a "property" interest in his or her contract and cannot be discharged summarily and arbitrarily during the contractual term, just as a tenured faculty member has a "property" interest in tenure. A hearing must be held. The difference, of course, is that the probationary faculty member's property interest terminates automatically when the contract expires.

The University of Illinois president charged Dr. Koch with "conduct seriously prejudicial to the university through deliberate infraction of commonly accepted standards of morality" — one of the explicit criteria found in the university's tenure code for termination of tenure "for cause." The

---

56 As set forth in the preceding section, public institutions are controlled by the Fourteenth Amendment which precludes all branches and divisions of state government, including governmental administrative agencies, from impairing the exercise of a constitutional right. The situation is different but not completely different in private institutions because their tenure plans which almost always are held to be part of the faculty member's employment contract, invariably will include the provision: "Dismissal will not be used to restrain faculty members in their exercise of academic freedom of other rights of American citizens, such as freedom of speech." Of course, as set forth in the preceding section, remedies can vary. A successful faculty member in a public institution may be reinstated in case of a retaliatory dismissal, but one in a private institution may only be able to collect money damages for breach of contract because courts are most reluctant to order specific performance of a contract for personal services. Thus, in an important sense, professional job security in a private institution, from a legal point of view may be less than in a public college or university, unless the private institution is one with "a long and honorable tradition of academic freedom and tenure."

University Senate's Tenure Committee, composed of top-ranking administrative and faculty personnel, recommended unanimously that Dr. Koch be reprimanded but not discharged. The Board of Trustees refused to accept the recommendation and conducted their own hearing, after which the Board ordered that Dr. Koch be dismissed one year before the expiration of his six year contract. In his appeal to the courts, Dr. Koch claimed his First Amendment rights were at issue, because the sole accusation against him was that his views, as expressed in the *Daily Illini*, were repugnant to commonly accepted standards of morality and could be seen as encouraging immoral behavior among students. One of the chief functions of free speech (and academic freedom) is to present new ideas that might invite dispute or even stir people to anger. The Illinois courts, however ruled that there had been no violation of Dr. Koch's contractual rights because the court read the contract only to require certain procedural steps taken in good faith. Dr. Koch had been granted detailed procedural protections, including formal hearings and representation by counsel. The United States Supreme Court refused to review the case.[57]

Four years after denying a hearing to Dr. Koch, the Supreme Court of the United States materially changed the legal landscape for retaliation cases in *Pickering v. Board of Education*.[58] Marvin Pickering, an Illinois high school teacher, wrote a letter to the local town paper after a proposed tax increase for educational use had been defeated by the voters for a second time. Pickering attacked the way in which a previous voter-approved bond issue of $5,500,000 had been used for, in his opinion, unduly favoring athletics at the expense of education and criticized the Superintendent for attempting to prevent teachers from expressing themselves on school policies. Pickering was immediately dismissed by the board for publishing his views. Later, at a hearing, the board determined that Pickering's dismissal was justified because of several partially false statements in his letter and because his letter unjustifiably "impugned the motives, honesty, integrity, responsibility and competence of the board and school administrators," making Pickering's continued service "detrimental to the best interests of the school." Pickering sued claiming retaliatory discharge and that his letter was protected by the First Amendment. But, like Dr. Koch, he lost in the Illinois courts on the ground that when he accepted a position as a teacher in the public schools he obliged himself to refrain from making public statements about the school,

---

[57] Koch v. Board of Trustees, 187 N.E.2d 340, 343 (Ill. App. Ct. 1962), *cert. denied,* 375 U.S. 989 (1964), *but compare* Endress v. Brookdale Community College, 364 A.2d 1080 (N.J. 1976) (comments made by a faculty member, who also was the faculty advisor to the college's student newspaper, in an editorial printed in the college newspaper, receive full protection from First Amendment).

[58] 391 U.S. 563 (1968).

"which in the absence of such position he would have an undoubted right to engage in."[59]

The Supreme Court granted review and reversed the Illinois court, stating: "To the extent that the Illinois Supreme Court opinion may be read to suggest that teachers may constitutionally be compelled to relinquish the First Amendment rights they would otherwise enjoy as citizens to comment on matters of public schools in which they worked, it proceeds on a premise that has been unequivocally rejected."[60] The Supreme Court applied a "balancing test" stating that the "problem in any case is to arrive at a balance between the interest of a [faculty member] as a citizen, in commenting upon matters of public concern and the interests of the State, as an employer, in promoting the efficiency of the public services it performs through its employees."[61] The Court noted that "no question of maintaining either discipline by immediate superiors or harmony among co-workers is presented here."[62] It then applied the *New York Times v. Sullivan*[63] standard that eliminated much of libel law bringing the expressions under the First Amendment's protection, and ruled that even if some of Pickering's statements contained mistakes — in the absence of proof that they had been made intentionally or recklessly — they could not serve as a ground for his dismissal. Two crucial questions requiring affirmative answers before a faculty member's speech is protected by *Pickering* are (1) whether the expression is constitutionally protected expression on a matter of public concern, and if so, (2) whether *Pickering's* balance of factors weighs favorably on the side of the faculty member's expression.[64]

Pickering's first requirement — speech on a matter of public concern — was reaffirmed and explained in two later Supreme Court cases: *Givhan v.*

---

59 Pickering v. Board of Educ., 225 N.E.2d 1 (Ill. 1967).

60 Pickering v. Board of Educ., 391 U.S. 563, 568 (1968).

61 *Id*. at 568.

62 *Id*. at 570.

63 376 U.S. 254 (1964).

64 In Maples, 858 F.2d at 1553-54 (11th Cir. 1988), the Court of Appeals summarized Pickering's balance of factors that must be weighed when courts determine whether an adverse employment decision was justified:

> Pickering requires the Court to balance the rights of public employees to speak on matters of public concern with the government's need to maintain the efficient performance of the public service it provides. Although such a balancing must occur case-by-case, the Supreme Court has discussed a number of factors to be considered in the analysis. The Court should review the time, place, and manner of the speech as well as the context in which the dispute between the parties arose . . . . Other factors to be considered are "[w]hether the statement impairs discipline by superiors or harmony among coworkers, has a detrimental impact on close working relationships for which personal loyalty and confidence are necessary, or impedes the performance of the speaker's duties or interferes with the regular operation of the enterprise." In assessing these factors, this Court has recognized that the *entire document* [or entire speech] at issue must be weighed against its disruptive impact on the workplace. (Citations omitted.)

Western Line School District (1979)[65] and *Connick v. Myers* (1983).[66] Givhan, a public school teacher, in a series of private meetings with her principal, vigorously complained about school practices she considered racially discriminatory, and her contract was not renewed. She sued, claiming retaliation and that her remarks were constitutionally protected under *Pickering* because they were on a matter of public concern, even though communicated privately to the principal and not to the public at large, as did Pickering. In a unanimous opinion, the U.S. Supreme Court agreed, ruling that "neither the [First] Amendment itself nor our decisions indicate that . . . freedom [of speech] is lost to the public employee who arranges to communicate privately with his employer rather than to spread his views before the public."[67]

In *Connick v. Myers* the question was whether *Pickering's* balancing test could be applied by a federal court to public employees who communicate their views about office personnel matters only to members of the office staff. The Court said, "No." Myers, an assistant district attorney scheduled for an unwanted transfer to another office division, circulated a questionnaire to other assistant district attorneys, asking whether they were happy with office transfer policy, office morale, the lack of a grievance procedure, the level of confidence in supervisors, and whether employees felt pressured to work in political campaigns. She was immediately fired. She sued in federal court, claiming retaliation for her exercise of constitutionally protected freedom of speech and that her questionnaire was constitutionally protected under *Pickering* and *Givhan*. On review, the U.S. Supreme Court disagreed by a vote of 5 to 4, ruling that Myers could not pursue her case in federal court because (with one exception) the questions posed by Myers "do not fall under the rubric of matters of 'public concern.'" The Supreme Court stated that:

> [W]hen a public employee speaks not as a citizen upon
> matters of public concern, but instead as an employee upon
> matters only of personal interest, absent the most unusual

---

65 439 U.S. 410 (1979).

66 461 U.S. 138 (1983).

67 Although the Court held that private expression on an issue of public concern is subject to the same balance of factors the Court used in Pickering, in a footnote it stated:

Although the First Amendment's protection of government employees extends to private as well as public expression, striking the *Pickering* balance in each context may involve different considerations. When a teacher speaks publicly, it is generally the content of his statements that must be assessed to determine whether they "in any way either impeded the teacher's proper performance of his daily duties in the classroom . . . or interfered with the regular operations of the schools generally." Private expression, however, may in some situations bring additional factors to the *Pickering* calculus. When a government employee personally confronts his immediate superior, the employing agency's institutional efficiency may be threatened not only by the content of the employee's message but also by the manner, time, and place in which it is delivered. [439 U.S. at 415, n.4].

circumstances, a federal court is not the appropriate forum in which to review the wisdom of a personnel decision taken by a public agency allegedly in reaction [retaliation] to the employee's behavior.

The Supreme Court indicated that Myers' dismissal could not be litigated in a federal court because the questionnaire was devoted to matters of close personal interest. *Givhan* and *Connick v. Myers* indicate the constitutional necessity of distinguishing between faculty communications on matters of public concern, which receive First Amendment protection, and faculty communication on matters of private or personal concern, which do not receive First Amendment protection — a distinction that in no way depends upon whether the communication, itself, is made in public or private.[68] Thus, under *Pickering*, *Givhan* and *Connick v. Myers*, the plaintiff faculty member must satisfy the burden of proving that the expression addresses a matter of public concern and was a substantial dismissal factor; if those burdens are carried, then a court will apply *Pickering's* balance of factors to the expression, where the governmental employer must satisfy the burden of proof that the balance is in the employer's favor.[69]

Courts have drawn a wavering line between what constitutes a matter of public or private concern in an educational setting. Examples of "private" speech include speech that concerns internal administration of an educational system and personal grievances. In *Ballard v. Blount*,[70] a federal district court held that a faculty member's critical comments on salary levels, his course assignments, a proposed course syllabus, and tenure decisions involve "matters relating to internal college affairs rather than to matters of political or social import . . ." and will be considered "private" not "public" speech. In *Ferrara v. Mills*,[71] a teacher's complaints about the way in which course registration and course assignments occurred were ruled to be

---

68 Connick significantly changed the parameters within which public employees might dissent. "Within a year of Connick, five cases brought by college professors on Pickering grounds had all been lost by the professors." M. Olivas, THE LAW AND HIGHER EDUCATION 250 (1989). In one of them, Landrum v. Eastern Ky. Univ., 578 F. Supp. 241 (E.D. Ky. 1984) the court stated:

> In frankness, the court must state that it reads *Connick* as deliberately intended to narrow the scope of [the additional cases decided under *Pickering*], even though they were not expressly overruled. A careful study of all the decision leads to the inevitable conclusion that the First Amendment in the employment context is now to be more narrowly interpreted to give greater scope to the legitimate rights of governmental entities as employers, and also to reduce the burdens on the courts caused by the burgeoning of litigation initiated by the decision [*Pickering*] upon which plaintiff relies here.

69 *See, e.g.*, Starsky v. Williams, 353 F. Supp. 900 (D. Ariz. 1972), *aff'd*, 512 F.2d 109 (9th Cir. 1975), and Rampey v. Allen, 501 F.2d 1090 (10th Cir. 1974).

70 581 F. Supp. 160, 164 (N.D. Ga. 1983), *aff'd*, 734 F.2d 1480 (11th Cir. 1984), *cert. denied*, 469 U.S. 1086 (1984).

71 781 F.2d 1508, 1516 (11th Cir. 1986).

unprotected speech. In *Renfroe v. Kirkpatrick*,[72] a teacher's protestations expressing unwillingness to "job share" were ruled unprotected speech. Memoranda discussing teaching methods and criteria of evaluation have been characterized as unprotected speech.[73]

On the other hand, in *Connick v. Myers*, the Supreme Court held that even if a document —only one of the questionnaire's questions —"touch[es] upon matters of public concern in only a most limited sense," it should, to that extent, be considered constitutionally protected speech. The Supreme Court ruled in *Pickering* that a faculty member's speech directly affecting the quality of education in a given academic system or educational institution is protected speech. In *Maples v. Martin*,[74] a federal court ruled that an unauthorized report authored by several dissident faculty members and distributed to faculty, alumni students, some administrators and an accrediting agency, criticizing the Departmental Head's management style and various weaknesses in the curriculum, inadequate facilities, a low faculty-to-school ratio and the poor performance of Auburn University's graduates on the professional licensing exam for engineers — was "sincere in [its] efforts to alert the public to the conditions in Auburn's ME Department" and was protected speech. In *Honore v. Douglas*,[75] commentary about a law school's admissions policy and size of the student population was held to be protected speech. *Southside Public Schools v. Hill*[76] held that faculty expressions about failure to execute federally mandated programs for handicapped students is an issue of public concern. Faculty expressions about educational standards and accreditation were held to be protected speech on matters of public concern in *Johnson v. Lincoln University*.[77]

A final case, *Mt. Healthy Board of Education v. Doyle*,[78] completes the Supreme Court's development of the law in this area, and again, like *Connick v. Myers*, it reflects a considerable amount of judicial deference to governing boards in their handling of personnel matters. Hypothetically suppose a tenured faculty member of seven years' service at a public institution writes a series of articles published in the local newspaper condemning, in his or her view, the president and the governing board for a wide variety of decisions and actions affecting education and the public welfare (protected under *Pickering*). Now suppose the governing board immediately dismisses the faculty member for professional incompetence and neglect of duty, and later

---

[72] 722 F.2d 714, 715 (11th Cir. 1984), *cert. denied* 469 U.S. 823 (1984).

[73] Hesse v. Board of Educ., 848 F.2d 748, 752 (7th Cir. 1988).

[74] 858 F.2d 1546, 1553 (1988).

[75] 833 F.2d 565 (5th Cir. 1987).

[76] 827 F.2d 270, 273 (8th Cir. 1987).

[77] 776 F.2d 443 (3d Cir. 1985).

[78] 429 U.S. 274 (1977); *see* Note, *Free Speech And Impermissible Motive In The Dismissal Of Public Employees*, 89 YALE L.J. 376 (1979).

conducts a hearing, charging him or her only with: manifest and substantial neglect of duty; namely, violation of a published rule prohibiting repeated and unexcused failure to meet classes (eight consecutive days in the last year).[79] Assuming the charge is proved in a full due-process hearing before a Tenure Committee that recommended a lesser disciplinary action, nevertheless can the tenured faculty member legally be dismissed in such circumstances, or is the dismissal illegal because it really is a poorly disguised retaliation for publication of the articles on a matter of public concern and obviously protected under *Pickering*? And, in a subsequent lawsuit, which party — the tenured faculty member or the institution — should have the burden of proof regarding the claim of retaliation for exercising the constitutionally protected right? *Mt. Healthy* answered these questions in an opinion for the Court by then Justice Rehnquist[80]:

> Initially, in this case, the burden was properly placed upon ... [the faculty member] to show that his conduct was constitutionally protected, and that this conduct was a "substantial factor" — or to put it in other words, that it was a "motivating factor" in the board's decision . . . [The Faculty member] having carried that burden, however, the district court should have gone on to determine whether the board had shown by preponderance of the evidence that it would have reached the same decision as to ... [the faculty member's] employment even in the absence of the protected conduct.

Thus, to confront the hypothetical problem, assuming the tenured faculty member demonstrated (1) that publication of the articles were on a matter of public concern and constitutionally protected under *Pickering*, and (2) that their publication was a motivating factor in the board's decision to dismiss him, a court would then apply *Mt. Healthy* and rule on the hypothetical problem by upholding the tenured faculty member's dismissal, so long as the board shows, as it can, that it had another, separate ground (manifest and substantial neglect of duty evidenced by repeated failure to meet classes on eight days) on which it could have independently based its decision to dismiss.

---

79 In Prebble v. Brodrick, 535 F.2d 605 (10th Cir. 1975), the tenured faculty member's dismissal for neglect of duty was upheld by the court after the faculty member admitted he "did not conduct any of this three classes on eight different dates ... some absences occurred while he was interviewing for a new position and some while he was elk hunting").

80 *Id.* at 287. *Mt. Healthy* was first applied to an institution of higher learning in *Franklin v. Atkins*, 562 F.2d 1188 (10th Cir. 1977), rejecting Bruce Franklin's claim that when the Board of Regents refused him a faculty position at the University of Colorado, it relied on constitutionally protected activities that he had engaged in while at Stanford University.

Does *Mt. Healthy's* legal doctrine invites governing board attorneys to search a faculty member's record for any acceptable ground that would justify a decision to terminate after the faculty member may have publicly attacked strongly-held societal beliefs or embarrassed the institution's governing authorities by an exercise of constitutionally protected freedom of speech or academic freedom? It is noteworthy that few cases exist in which courts have ruled against the institution's ground because the institution did not carry its burden, and almost all of them are cases in which the institution's ground has been hastily conceived and undermined by evidence presented by the faculty member such that the institution's dismissal ground was not fully supported by "substantial evidence."[81]

What accounts for *Mt. Healthy's* rule is a concern by the Supreme Court: If a public employee became aware of his or her possible discharge, then that employee might immediately rush out to the nearest media source and exercise First Amendment rights, making statements highly critical of his or her agency and its administrators; the employee thereafter could claim that any subsequent discharge was based on those public statements, and was illegal because it interfered with the employee's constitutional right to free speech.[82] Thus, "the Court's [concern in *Mt. Healthy*] is on activities intentionally undertaken by the plaintiff [the dismissed faculty member] that

---

[81] *See e.g.,* Hale v. Walsh, 747 P.2d 1288 (Idaho Ct. App. 1987) in which the faculty member demonstrated that his action and expression (e.g., a letter protesting policies of special treatment of a student, alleging it was done because the student was the son-in-law of a Dean Emeritus) was protected by the First Amendment and that it was a motivating factor in the administrative decision to dismiss him. Thereafter, the defendants, a Dean and a Vice President, claimed under Mt. Healthy, according to the court, that:

> they showed — by a preponderance of the evidence — that their recommendation [of dismissal] was based on the following conduct: a pattern of harassing students seeking his aid and guidance; disharmony within the history department; the detrimental effect on the working relationships between the Colleges of Liberal Arts and Education due to Hale's conduct with students and faculty; and a weak department promotion committee report.
>
> While [defendants] presented evidence in support of these reasons, the evidence was rebutted. Hale presented evidence showing he was a good teacher and had a good relationship with students. Evidence was also presented showing an improvement in the harmony within the history department after Hale arrived. Hale also submitted proof he was the only faculty member recommended for a promotion who was not rehired.

The jury found in favor of Hale, the faculty member, which the court accepted saying that the jury's "verdict is supported by substantial and competent, albeit conflicting evidence." *See also,* Daulton v. Affeldt, 678 F.2d 487 (4th Cir. 1982).

[82] The Supreme Court stated in Mt. Healthy (429 U.S. at 285-86):

> The difficulty with the rule enunciated by the District Court is that it would require reinstatement in cases where a dramatic and perhaps abrasive incident is inevitably on the minds of those responsible for [the employment decision], and does indeed play a part in that decision — even if the same decision would have been reached had the incident not occurred. .... [the employee] ought not be able, by engaging in such conduct, to prevent his employer from assessing his performance second, simply because the protected conduct makes the employer more certain of the correctness of its decision.

could make the plaintiff 'better off' than he would be 'had he done nothing.' . . . the Court is [concerned with] an *event or transaction* that the plaintiff engaged in, which then influenced the employer's response."[83]

It may be argued that the *Mt. Healthy* rule invites subterfuge and possible employer abuse. However, there are reported decisions in which courts have redressed genuine cases of employer retaliation. For example, in *Goss v. San Jacinto Junior College*,[84] the board refused to renew plaintiff Goss' contract of employment. Before non-renewal, Mrs. Goss sought to organize a chapter of the National Faculty Association (NFA), and the college's president distributed by campus mail a newsletter to all faculty expressing his concerns about the organization, while denying proponents of the NFA to distribute literature by campus mail. When her husband filed his candidacy for a seat on the Board of Regents, Mrs. Goss was advised by her departmental chair "to have her husband withdraw from the election." She claimed the decision not to renew her contract was in retaliation for exercising her constitutionally protected political and union activities under the First Amendment,[85] and sued for money damages. The college's defense was *Mt. Healthy's* rule; that Mrs. Goss had her contract non-renewed because of poor evaluations of her teaching and declining enrollment. But, the president stated openly he had recommended Mrs. Goss' contract not be renewed to discipline her for "creating or trying to create ill will or lack of cooperation . . . with the administration." Additionally, the court stated that the evaluation of Mrs. Goss' teaching "was inconsistent with the objective criteria established for the rating," having improperly not been awarded credits to which she was entitled, which, if awarded "would have ranked [her] in the middle of the seventeen history instructors rather than in the bottom three." Thus, this case is one in which there was no substantial evidence supporting the governing board's grounds for discharge. After trial, a jury agreed with Mrs. Goss awarding her $23,400 in back pay. The U.S. Court of Appeals for the 5th

---

83 Blumrosen, *Society In Transition II: Price Waterhouse And The Individual Employment Discrimination Case*, 42 RUTGERS LAW REV. 1023, 1036 (1990). (Emphasis in original.)

84 588 F.2d 96 (5th Cir. 1979), *also see* Cooper v. Ross, 472 F. Supp. 802 (E.D. Ark. 1979) (The University of Arkansas at Little Rock refused to renew Cooper's, a non-tenured faculty member's, contract because of allegedly deficient professional competence, and he sued, alleging retaliation: "The University demonstrated that there were weaknesses in Cooper's performance as a teacher," but the "court is convinced however, that these weaknesses would not have resulted in the non-reappointment decision had Cooper not joined the PLP [Progressive Labor Party] and publicly acknowledged his communist beliefs." Two months before he joined the PLP, Cooper's only faculty evaluation rated him "average or superior in every category," and "[m]oreover, as noted by the ad hoc faculty committee, the reasons originally given for the [non-renewal] decision were ambiguous and poorly substantiated." The University failed to carry its Mt. Healthy burden, while Cooper carried his, and won); *also see* Greenwood v. Ross, 778 F.2d 448 (8th Cir. 1985).

85 Although public governing boards need not engage in collective bargaining with faculty organizations in the absence of a law so requiring, it is settled that faculty members have a constitutional right to organize, McLaughlin v. Telendis, 398 F.2d 287 (7th Cir. 1968).

Circuit reviewed the case, and affirmed saying: "There was ample evidence to support the jury finding that Mrs. Goss had not been hired 'because of her political and/or professional activities,'" and "there was sufficient evidence to support the jury finding that 'matters other than Mrs. Goss' political and or professional activities' were not responsible for the board of regents action.[86]"

In summary of the current state of the law applying to retaliation cases, the Supreme Court has created a four-pronged, or four-stepped, legal doctrine controlling dismissals of tenured faculty members in cases where the faculty member claims his or her dismissal was not *bona fide* but was in retaliation for the faculty member's exercise of academic freedom or a constitutional right, and then sues in a court:

First: The faculty member must to the court's satisfaction meet the burden of demonstrating that the faculty member's action or speech was on a matter of public concern, and protected by academic freedom or by a constitutional right such as free speech. (This is a question of law for a judge to decide.) *and*

Second: The faculty member must also meet to the satisfaction of the trier of fact that the additional burden of demonstrating that his or her protected action or speech was a substantial, or motivating factor in his or her dismissal. (This is a question of fact to be decided by a jury, or by a judge if there is no jury in the case.) *then even if the expression is constitutionally protected and a motivating factor,*

Third: The institution's governing board must fail in a court's judgment to meet its burden under *Pickering's* balancing test, failing to show that its decision was justified because the balance weighs in favor of the governmental board's need to maintain the efficient performance of the educational service it provides which is materially impaired by the faculty member's speech. (This is a question of law for the judge to decide.) *then,*

Fourth: Only if the faculty member carries the first two burdens and the governing board fails to pass *Pickering's* balancing test, must the college or university's governing board come forward and satisfactorily meet *Mt. Healthy's* burden of demonstrating, by a preponderance of the evidence, that the board would have taken the same

---

[86]   *Id.*

action absent the protected activity, which if it fails to do, entitles
the faculty member to prevail. (This is a question of fact for a jury
to decide when a case has a jury.)

Finally, under *Mt. Healthy*, when judges make their decisions about whether
the burdens have been carried, they must always bear in mind that it "is
equally well established that . . . it is not the function of a federal [or state]
court to second guess the decision of an official of a state university on
matters within his discretion which do not rise to the level of a constitutional
deprivation."[87]

The tenured faculty member failed to satisfy the first burden of showing
that she had engaged in protected speech in *Roseman v. Indiana University
of Pennsylvania*.[88] An associate professor complained that her contract was
wrongfully not renewed in retaliation because she complained to the dean,
and later to the faculty at a departmental meeting, about alleged improprieties
in the way in which the departmental head was handling the selection process
for a new department chair. She claimed her complaints were constitutionally protected speech under the First Amendment. The court disagreed. It
distinguished the scope of *Pickering's* application as not applying to this
case, and rejected the faculty member's claim because: (1) her comments
"were essentially private communications in which only members [of the
department and the dean] had any interest, whereas Pickering's letter was a
public communication on a matter of public interest; and (2) her comments
had a "potentially disruptive impact on the functioning of the department"
because they "called into question the integrity of . . . [the departmental
chair], whereas Pickering's letter was not directed to any person with whom
he normally worked and had no disruptive impact." The court "concluded
that the plaintiff's [Roseman's] communications fall outside the First
Amendment's protections."

In *Ollman v. Toll*[89] the faculty member failed to satisfy the second
burden (if the speech or activity is constitutionally protected, then the faculty
member must show causation; namely, that the speech was a substantial, or

---

87   Ollman v. Toll, 518 F. Supp. 1196, 1202 (D. Md. 1981), (citing Shaw v. Board of Trustees, 549
F.2d 929, 932 (4th Cir. 1976)).

88   520 F. 2d 1364 (3d Cir. 1975), *and see* Jawa v. Fayetteville State Univ., 426 F. Supp. 218
(E.D.N.C. 1976), *but compare* the court's approach in Mayberry v. Dees, 663 F.2d 502, 519 (4th Cir.
1981) (rejecting Roseman's characterization and indicating that a similar communication would
receive First Amendment protection).

89   518 F. Supp. 1196 (D. Md. 1981), *aff'd*, 704 F. 2d 139 (4th Cir. 1983). *Also see* Mayberry v.
Dees, 663 F.2d 502 (4th Cir. 1981) (faculty member established that his communication was
protected but failed to establish that his denial of tenure was motivated, at least in part, by his
communication), and Leachman v. Rector, Univ. of Va., 691 F. Supp. 961 (W.D. Va. 1988) (faculty
librarian failed to show that communication with joint legislative audit and review commission was
a motivating factor in dismissal).

motivating, factor in the decision). Bertell Ollman, a tenured Marxist, political science professor at New York University, after a nationwide search, had been recommended in late February by the Search Committee along with Robert J. Holt, a professor at the University of Minnesota, to the University of Maryland's Provost, Murray L. Polakoff, for appointment as Chairman of the Department of Political Science. In a later meeting with the Provost, the Search Committee members urged that Dr. Ollman be selected whereupon Provost Polakoff agreed. After reviewing the matter with Chancellor Gluckstern and after receiving his concurrence, Provost Polakoff telephoned Dr. Ollman, and offered him the post, provided the University's President ultimately approved the appointment. Dr. Ollman accepted. More than six weeks elapsed before Chancellor Gluckstern forwarded the appointing papers to President Elkins who was slated to retire at the end of June. "The publicity evoked considerable comment by both public officials and private citizens, and the Ollman matter quite rapidly became a cause célèbre." "President Elkins left office without having acted on the appointment."

The University of Maryland's newly appointed President, John S. Toll, reopened the whole matter, personally took control, and personally made a thoroughly painstaking review of the entire process, the candidate and his qualifications, seeking new sources of information, without inquiring in any way about Marxism or Dr. Ollman's beliefs. However, he obviously was aware of the situation he was confronting. President Toll refused to appoint Dr. Ollman. Claiming retaliation, Dr. Ollman filed suit arguing that the First Amendment protected his Marxist beliefs and that they were a substantial and motivating factor in the University president's decision not to appoint him. The court agreed that Dr. Ollman's Marxist beliefs were constitutionally protected but disagreed that they had been a motivating or substantial factor in President Toll's decision:

> The evidence in this case indicates that the reasons assigned by President Toll in his statement of July 20 and in his testimony were the true motivating factors for his decision. President Toll did not base his decision on plaintiff's Marxist beliefs. Rather, he acted as he did because it was his considered judgment that plaintiff did not possess the qualifications to develop the Department of Government and Politics in the manner in which President Toll thought it should develop.

> The evidence indicates that the reasons assigned by President Toll for his decision were sincere ones, that there was an adequate factual basis for the conclusions reached and that he had fairly and conscientiously reviewed the

entire matter before reaching his decision. Whether or not this Court might agree with President Toll concerning the direction which the Department should take and the qualifications of a Chairman to lead the Department in that direction, it is not for this Court to substitute its judgment for that of the University's Chief Executive Officer, so long as a legally impermissible reason was not the substantial or motivating factor.

The third of the law's four prongs, or steps, is illustrated by a case in which the governing board carried its burden under *Pickering's* balancing test by showing that a faculty member's speech, although constitutionally protected, was outweighed by the governing board's interest in maintaining the efficient performance of the educational service it provides. In *Franklin v. Stanford University*,[90] the University agreed that, although private, Stanford should be treated as though it were a public university for purposes of this case. Bruce Franklin, a tenured associate professor of English, was dismissed for his role in four anti-Vietnam War incidents: (1) for participating in disruptive conduct which prevented Ambassador Henry Cabot Loge from speaking on campus; (2) for having "urged and incited students and other[s] . . . to [disrupt University functions] and specifically to shut down a University computer facility;" (3) for significantly interfering with a police order to disperse by inciting those present to ignore it, after having shut down the computer facility; and (4) for having "intentionally urged and incited students and other persons to engage in conduct calculated to disrupt activities of the University . . . and which threatened injury to individuals and property." All of this activity and speech involved a dismissal for speech and activity about public, not private, matters under the *Pickering/Connick* analysis and it clearly was a motivating factor in the dismissal decision; so, the court applied *Pickering's* balancing test. It ruled that the faculty member's free speech interest was outweighed by the governing board's interests:

> It is clear that the constitutional freedom to speak does not
> license a teacher to substantially disrupt and interfere with

---

90 218 Cal. Rptr. 228 (Cal. Ct. App. 1985); *see also*, Hesse v. Board of Educ., 848 F.2d 748 (7th Cir. 1988) (governing board's interest in rectifying deteriorating employment relationship which had been five years developing justified weighing Pickering's balance of factors in favor of the board); Connick v. Myers, 461 U.S. 138, 152 (1983) (because governmental employers must act to avert impending crises, the closeness of the proximity (or the probability of) future disruption may be considered), and Maples v. Martin, 858 F.2d 1546 (11th Cir. 1988) (free speech interests of dissident faculty member in the publication and circulation of a report critical of Engineering Department's methods and practices of education held outweighed under Pickering by the board's interest in transferring tenured faculty member to another division of the University in order to eliminate divisiveness).

the normal operations of his or her employer, whether they be instruction, research, or administration. Expressive conduct which may not justify criminal or civil liability may be the subject of employer discipline. Plaintiff's expressive conduct in our view was well out of constitutional bounds. Speech which results in disruption, which materially interferes with school activities, or impairs discipline is not constitutionally protected against an employer's response.

On the other hand, *Rampey v. Allen*[91] is an example in which the *Pickering* balance was struck in favor of the faculty members. The Oklahoma College of the Liberal Arts abolished tenure but "some of the plaintiffs [tenured and non-tenured faculty members] had never been notified that tenure had been abolished," and both facts occasioned considerable discussion. The faculty members involved used an interdisciplinary approach to teaching, and were considered to be part of the core curriculum teaching staff. President Carter recommended to the Board that they be dismissed, the Board members "accepted this recommendation, and in carrying it out gave no reasons for their action." The faculty members sued, alleging retaliation for exercise of constitutional rights.

In court, the faculty members proved their expression was protected and a motivating factor in their dismissal. President Carter sought to tilt *Pickering's* balance in the institution's favor. He testified that the faculty members were dismissed because they were "divisive," and explained what he meant by "divisive." Dean Ledgerwood was "divisive" because "on one occasion the Dean defended another faculty member's right to criticize the administration." Faculty member Papplean was considered "divisive" because he characterized President Carter as "a three-time loser" following "Carter's having been outvoted by the majority of the students in three controversial campus issues." Maness was considered "divisive" because he told another faculty member that Carter "could not communicate." Wimbish was considered "divisive" because "he spent too much time during the final two weeks of the semester talking to students in the dining hall." Bolton was "divisive" because "he had sought clarification as to the scope of his duties as director of personnel." Poole was "divisive" because she declared: "We live in different worlds; we live in different atmospheres; we have different philosophies." Carter also found the faculty members "divisive and uncooperative" because "they failed to join certain organizations, such as the Oklahoma Educational Association . . . ." There also was "evidence to

---

91 501 P.2d 1090 (10th Cir. 1974)

establish that the group as a whole was 'divisive' because they associated together."

Rejecting the institution's reliance on *Pickering* as justification for the dismissals, the court stated that "the record fails to disclose that [the faculty members'] activities were in any way excessive or unduly burdensome to the school" and that:

> In the last analysis, it was the [faculty members'] refusal to conform to President Carter's patterns and molds, all of which were personal and subjective on his part, which was the cause of their being fired. Surely the right to be free from this kind of personality control is a constitutionally protected right under the First Amendment since it is a species of expression. One had to become a person who was in his image and likeness if he or she wished to serve as a member of the faculty at OCLA. By his own testimony Carter is shown to have been jealous of his power and insecure in his position as well as unable to tolerate any dissent, criticism or disagreement, all of which he called "divisiveness." Yet there is no evidence that the appellants constituted any threat to the operation of the college — to Carter personally, perhaps, but not the college.

> The evidence supported the view that the [faculty members'] classes were well regarded by the students. Consider, for example, the classes of appellant Holt about whom Carter stated "He would not and could not do his job" and he "didn't fit into the atmosphere of the college at all." At the same time, the students voted him the outstanding teacher of the year in 1969 and requested that he be the commencement speaker that year. . . . While a college president is entitled to respect and authority within his sphere, this does not extend to the exercise of absolute control over the associations and expressions of the faculty members. . . .

A final case illustrates *Mt. Healthy's* fourth legal requirement. *Hickingbottom v. Easley*[92] is another illustration of a successful case brought

---

[92] 494 F. Supp. 980 (1980), *and see*, Stern v. Shouldice, 706 F.2d 742 (1983) (evidence sustained jury finding that college officials were motivated to dismiss tenured faculty member in retaliation for his constitutionally protected speech advising a student to seek legal advice about the student's suspension. Jury rejected as unproven the college official's claim based on Mt. Healthy that the faculty member inadequately investigated the situation before giving his advice and that showed he lacked the deliberative qualities necessary for professional competence).

by a faculty member. Hickingbottom was a non-tenured professor having received nine one-year contracts, and had served seven years as a departmental chair in Phillips County Community College. There was no written policy, but at a faculty meeting where Hickingbottom was present, President Easley reviewed some recent problems caused by communications with off-campus persons, and then "demanded that [the faculty] follow the [internal] chain of command before writing any letters [to outside persons] concerning college problems." Thereafter, Hickingbottom wrote a confidential letter to the State Division Of Motor Vehicles indicating that he had repeatedly seen two cars on campus for two years carrying dealer tags; that this "practice not only evades sales tax and tag fees but local assessment as well," and asked for an "investigation and correction" of this matter. "The cars had been furnished to President Easley and his wife to increase their compensation, as they were receiving the maximum salaries allowed by law."

A police officer came onto campus and asked President Easley where he might find Hickingbottom. "While conversing with the officer . . . President Easley learned of the contents of [Hickingbottom's] letter by reading it over the officer's shoulder." Thereafter, President Easley wrote Hickingbottom that his contract would not be renewed because Hickingbottom "had been uncooperative with him and his staff," because he "was not maintaining the proper relationship with his students, and [because] he had followed disruptive procedure designed to harm the College." Two of the three charges were based on Hickingbottom's letter, and the remaining one was not established. Hickingbottom sued, claiming his contract non-renewal was in retaliation for exercising a constitutionally protected right. The court agreed:

> The Court is of the opinion from the record in this case, in view of the limited circumstances as described by the record, that it was not permissible for the defendants to summarily discharge the plaintiff or to deny the plaintiff a renewal of his contract solely on the basis of his act of reporting an actual violation to state law prior to calling it to the attention of certain persons in the chain of command listed in the President's announced Line Authority Policy. As already concluded herein, the plaintiff was exercising his First Amendment rights in reporting to appropriate officials an obvious violation of the law. The Court further concludes that this protected action of the plaintiff was a "substantial or motivating factor" in the decision to deny the plaintiff reappointment as a member of the faculty for another year. The Court is of the opinion that the plaintiff met his burden as required by law, but the College has failed to meet its burden by a preponderance of the evidence that the same non-reappointment decision would

have been made absent Hickingbottom's exercise of First
Amendment rights.

An important conclusion clearly emerges from the discussions of the law
in this section. Whatever might be one's view of the adequacy of the
Pickering/Connick/Givhan/Mt. Healthy line of cases and their progeny, in
creating the law applicable to retaliatory discharges these cases do not
demonstrate that the concept of tenure impedes or impairs institutions of
higher education from dismissing tenured faculty members because of a
demonstrated lack of professional competence or dishonesty, or because of
manifest and substantial neglect of professional duties. Properly understood,
the law controlling retaliatory discharge provides extremely strong grounds
for concluding that in the area of retaliatory dismissals, the legal aspects of
tenure do not unacceptably impair institutions of higher learning from
achieving their proper educational goals.

F. Judicial Review Of Institutional Decisions Dismissing Tenured Faculty Members Alleging Due Process Violations

This section will not canvass all cases involving claims to procedural
requirements, but seeks to present the critical structures of due process of
law. In a landmark case, *Perry v. Sindermann*,[93] the U.S. Supreme Court
ruled that a tenured faculty member at a public institution has a "property"
interest protected by the Fourteenth Amendment and that the property
interest can be taken away by government only if the faculty member first has
been afforded full procedural "due process of law."[94] Although "[d]ue

---

[93] 408 U.S. 593 (1972), *see* text *supra* at note 45. In Goldberg v. Kelly, 397 U.S. 254, 255 (1970),
the Court ruled that a public welfare recipient had a property interest in continued receipt of benefits
and that New York could not terminate "public assistance payments to a particular recipient without
affording him [notice and] the opportunity for an evidentiary hearing prior to termination." Similarly
in Bell v. Burson, 402 U.S. 535, 539 (1971), the Court determined that a clergyman involved in an
automobile accident had a protected interest in his driver's license under state law, and thus had an
interest protected by due process of law.

[94] The situation is usually similar in private institutions, but faculty members sue to vindicate a
contractual, rather than property, interest, because a private institution's tenure rules and regulations
are almost always held by courts reasonably to be part of a tenured faculty member's employment
contract. *See* note 45, *supra*. Indeed, Courts will usually require both public and private institutions

process is a flexible concept, the very nature of which negates any concept of inflexible procedures universally applicable to every imaginable situation,"[95] once "it is determined that due process applies, the question remains what process is due" even though "all situations calling for procedural safeguards [do not] call for the same kind of procedure."[96] Two general requirements are clear. All courts agree that "due process" always requires, at minimum, adequately *specific notice of the charges* and an unbiased, fair and effective *hearing* at which to determine the validity of the charges.[97] The United States Supreme Court has not identified a "check list," or a bundle, of precise procedures, that must be afforded to all tenured faculty members in all dismissal cases. Beyond the absolute requirements of adequate notice and some kind of a fair and effective hearing, the Supreme Court has stated only that further required "due process" procedures will vary from situation to situation, to be determined on a case-by case basis, with court decisions

---

to comply with their own stated procedures, holding them to be part of the employment contract. For example, in Skehan v. Board of Trustees of Bloomsburg State College, 501 F.2d 31 (3d Cir. 1976), a nonrenewed professor alleged that the college had not complied with its own policies providing for a hearing in academic freedom cases. The Court of Appeals ruled that the college must follow its own policy on academic freedom if, on remand, the trial court found (1) that the policy granted a right to a hearing under state contract law, and (2) that this case involved academic freedom within the meaning of the policy. After remand and a second appeal, the Court of Appeals further ruled that the professor did have a contract right to the procedures specified in the institution's policy statement and that the college had violated the professor's procedural rights. 590 F.2d 470 (3d Cir. 1978). In addition, public institutions also are often subject to state statutes or administrative regulations establishing procedures applicable to faculty personnel decisions. *See, e.g.*, Brouillete v. Board of Directors, 519 F.2d 126 (8th Cir. 1975), and compare the reverse situation found in Rutcosky v. Board of Trustees, 545 P.2d 567 (Wash. 1976).

[95]   Thomas v. Ward, 529 F.2d 916, 919 (4th Cir. 1975).

[96]   Morrissey v. Brewer, 408 U.S. 471, 481 (1972).

[97]   *See, e.g.*, State v. McPhee, 94 N.W.2d 711, 716 (Wis. 1959) where Wisconsin's Supreme Court emphasized that "the cardinal and ultimate test of the presence or absence of due process of law in any administrative proceeding is the presence or absence of the 'rudiments of fair play long known to our law,'" and McLendon v. Morton, 249 S.E. 2d 919 (W.Va. 1978) where a West Virginia court determined that a faculty member denied tenure had been deprived of a property interest because Parkersburg Community College's published eligibility criteria for tenure included an "objective" statement that tenure was acquired after completion of six years as a full-time teaching member of the faculty at the rank of assistant professor. McLendon met both criteria. She applied for tenure, and was rejected on grounds of competence. The court ruled that satisfaction of the two criteria created a sufficient interest such that "she could not be denied tenure on the basis of her competence without some procedural due process" which, at a minimum, necessitated notice of the specific reasons for removal and a hearing before an unbiased tribunal at which McLendon would have a fair opportunity to refute the issues raised in the notice of specific charges. *Compare*, Beitzel v. Jeffrey, 643 F.2d 870 (1st Cir. 1981), and Goodisman v. Lytle, 724 F.2d 818 (9th Cir. 1984).

depending upon the weight of the factors found in the following balancing formula:[98]

> . . . th[is] Court has spoken sparingly about the requisite procedures. [Our] decisions underscore the truism that [d]ue process, unlike some legal rules, is not a technical conception with a fixed content unrelated to time, place and circumstances. *[Due process] is flexible and calls for such procedural protections as the particular situation demands.* . . . our prior decisions indicate that identification of the specific dictates of due process generally requires consideration of three distinct factors: First, the private [faculty member's] interest that will be affected by the official action; second, the risk or an erroneous deprivation of such interest through the procedures used, and the probable value, if any, of additional or substitute procedural safeguards; and finally, the Government's interest, including the function involved and the fiscal and administrative burdens that additional or substitute procedural requirements would entail.

1. *Loudermill's* Pre-Termination Hearing Requirement

Although the exact contours of all legally required procedures for ultimate tenure hearings remain to be worked out under the balancing test on a case-by-case basis, administrators and governing boards should be carefully aware that the Supreme Court's *Loudermill*[99] decision is quite specific. It requires that certain procedural safeguards be afforded a tenured faculty member *before* even temporary removal from the classroom, library or laboratory, even though salary and fringe benefits may continue,[100] and even though an adequate, due-process proceeding necessarily will occur later.

---

[98] Mathews v. Eldridge, 425 U.S. 319 (1976). For criticism of this balancing test *see*, Mashaw, *The Supreme Court's Due Process Calculus For Administrative Adjudication In Mathews v. Eldridge*, 44 U. CHI. L. REV. 28 (1976).

[99] *See* text at note 46, *supra*.

[100] Some courts have expressly required a hearing before a decision is made terminating a faculty member's pay or other substantial employment benefits. For example, in Skehan v. Board of Trustees of Bloomburg State College, 501 F.2d 31 (3d Cir. 1974), a pre-Loudermill case, the faculty member was relieved of duties, dismissed and removed from the payroll for three months before the ultimate hearing was held. The Court held that because of its late timing, the hearing did not meet due process of law requirements. On the other hand, in Chung v. Park, 514 F.2d 382 (3d Cir. 1975), the court upheld the due-process validity of a hearing provided before job benefits were terminated but after the decision to terminate was made. Presumably, these cases would be controlled by Loudermill's requirements today.

2. Due Process

In *Ferguson v. Thomas*,[101] the Court of Appeals for the Fifth Circuit enunciated a widely accepted but generalized statement of "minimal" due process protections — two relating to "notice" and two relating to the "hearing" — to which a tenured professor is entitled before he or she may be dismissed. Details of the protections must be fleshed out by courts on a case-by-case basis or by colleges and universities in their own tenure codes.

> These minimum standards describe the boundaries within which the State has discretion to adopt the procedures it finds most appropriate. These include the right of a professor to: (1) be advised of the cause for his termination in sufficient detail so as to enable him to show any error that may exist; (2) be advised of the names and the nature of the testimony of the witnesses against him; (3) a meaningful opportunity to be heard in his own defense within a reasonable time; and (4) a hearing before a tribunal that possesses some academic expertise and an apparent impartiality toward the charges.

a. Notice

"Notice" is one of the two basic elements of due process of law. "The notice which must be given must afford [the faculty member] 'a reasonable opportunity to know the claims of the opposing party and to meet them.'"[102]

The constitutional validity of a particular notice mechanism turns on whether it is "reasonably calculated, under all of the circumstances, to apprise interested parties of the pendency of the action [e.g., the specifics of the complaint in a tenure hearing] and afford them an opportunity to present

---

[101] 430 F.2d 852 (5th Cir. 1970), *and see* Stewart v. Bailey, 556 F.2d 281 (1977) *and also* Levitt v. University of Tex. El Paso, 759 F.2d 1224 (1985). In Poterma v. Ping, 462 F.Supp. 388 (E.D. Ohio 1978) a tenured economics professor at Ohio University claimed a denial of due process after being dismissed for failure to perform faculty duties and for inability to communicate with students. The court ruled generally that the faculty member was entitled to the following, minimum due process safeguards: (1) a written notice specifically stating the grounds for the proposed dismissal; (2) adequate notice of a hearing on the validity of the grounds for the proposed dismissal; (3) a fair hearing at which the faculty member has an opportunity to submit evidence and controvert that evidence against him, and the grounds for dismissal; and (4) a final statement of the grounds; that is findings of fact plus conclusions with their supporting reasons, for dismissal, should it occur. *Also see*, Riggins v. Regents Univ. of Neb., 790 F.2d 707, 712 (8th Cir. 1986), and Bowling v. Scott, 587 F.2d 229 (5th Cir. 1979).

[102] White v. Board of Trustees, 648 P.2d 528, 535 (Wyo. 1982), (quoting Morgan v. United States, 304 U.S. 1, 18 (1938).)

their objections."[103] Courts tend to follow the maxim: the greater the importance of the interest at stake, the greater the certainty must be that the particular notice was clear, specific and actually effective. The "require-ments of the law are met where the notice given the [faculty member] is not misleading and apprises him or her of the issues in controversy, . . . and [the faculty member is] not subjected to surprise."[104] To eliminate surprise a faculty member should be "advised long before the hearing of his right to the names of witnesses" against him; of his right to interview them, and of his right to "take advantage of discovery procedures available."[105]

Notice controls the whole tenure hearing process, providing a frame-work for the hearing and governing the actions of the parties and the tribunal. A Board was held to violate a faculty member's rights because its reasons for its final decision were changed from the reasons given at the time of the Board's initial decision to nonrenew. The faculty member received "no notice of the [additional] items and was thus not able to prepare a defense to them at the hearing." As "such the essential elements of due process were not met." The faculty member was "entitled to be judged solely on the reasons enunciated in the notice of nonrenewal. Due process requires no less."[106] Moreover, "a violation of Federal due process [also will occur] insofar as [a tenured faculty member's] discharge [is] based on standards of academic freedom narrower than the standards noticed in the charge."[107]

The tenure codes of colleges and universities, or state statutes or administrative law rules, may include a provision to the effect that "materials in personnel files of faculty members which may serve as a basis for affecting the status of their employment are to be made available for inspection by the faculty member at his or her request; information of a derogatory nature shall not be entered or filed unless the faculty member is given notice and an opportunity to copy, to review and to comment on them; a faculty member shall have the right to enter, and have attached to any such derogatory statement, his own comments thereon, and such material shall not be used in

---

103 Mullane v. Central Hanover Bank & Trust Co., 339 U.S. 306, 314 (1950), *see also* Armstrong v. Manzo, 380 U.S. 545, 550 (1965).

104 White v. Board of Trustees, 648 P.2d 528, 535 (Wyo. 1982).

105 *Id.*

106 Haddock v. Board of Educ., 661 P.2d 368, 377 (Kan. 1983).

107 Starsky v. Williams, 353 F. Supp. 900, 927 (D. Ariz. 1972). ("Looking at the evidence as a whole insofar as it reflects the sum and substance of six years as a member of the faculty, an acknowledged and respected teacher and scholar, and a man with national visibility; and after carefully studying all the evidence which the Board of Regents [of Arizona State University] had before it as a basis for its action, the isolated incidents that could reasonably lead to some disciplinary action were of such a minor nature or so long ago, and the major emphasis in the charges is so clearly based on protected ideology, that this Court must conclude that the primary reason for the discipline of Professor Starsky is grounded in his exercise of his First Amendment rights in expressing unpopular views.").

any proceeding against the faculty member without first informing him or her of its intended use and giving the faculty member a fair opportunity to copy and to review the material." This type of provision directly relates to the "notice" requirement, and to the elimination of surprise at a Tenure Hearing. It "means that [a faculty member] has the right to know within a reasonable time any of the derogatory evidence, oral or written, that would be used against him at the hearing before the Board or Commission."[108]

Due process requires specific charges reasonably related to professional competence. Adequate due-process notice of the charges requires that they not be vague. They must be written, given directly to the faculty member, and formulated in clear, precise and specific language. The due process prohibition of vagueness is really a due process requirement of definiteness in the prescription of dismissal charges. It demands adequately specific and complete language that conveys "sufficiently definite warning as to the proscribed conduct when measured by common understandings and practices."[109] A charge that is vague, abstract and indefinite not only violates due process in the sense that it fails to give fair notice, thereby fostering surprise at a hearing because it disallows a faculty member from preparing every competent defense,[110] but it also violates due process in the sense that it neither adequately guides nor sufficiently governs the conduct of the hearing, itself, by the hearing panel and by the Governing Board, and thereby encourages arbitrary, capricious or erratic decisionmaking.[111] The due process proscription against vagueness has "special bite in the First Amendment area."[112]

The due-process requirement of a reasonable relationship between the charge and one's professional competencies is illustrated by *Board of Regents v. Martine*.[113] A tenured faculty member was dismissed for "dishonesty and moral turpitude" for acts related to his off-campus administration of a health insurance program for students. Although there was

---

[108] Cockburn v. Santa Monica Community College, 207 Cal. Rptr. 589 (Cal. Ct. App. 1984).

[109] Jordan v. DeGeorge, 341 U.S. 223 (1951), *also see*, Coates v. Cincinnati, 402 U.S. 611 (1971) and Papachristou v. Jacksonville, 405 U.S. 156 (1976). On a number of occasions the U.S. Supreme Court has ruled:

> [A law] which either forbids or requires the doing of an act in terms so vague that men of common intelligence must necessarily guess at its meaning and differ as to its application, violates the first essential of due process of law.

Connally v. General Const. Co., 269 U.S. 385, 391 (1925), *also see*, Amsterdam, *The Void For Vagueness Doctrine In The Supreme Court*, 109 U. OF PA. L. REV. 67 (1960).

[110] "[D]ue process requires that there be an opportunity to present every available defense." American Surety Co. v. Baldwin, 287 U.S. 156, 168 (1932) (Brandeis, J.).

[111] *See* Starsky v. Williams, 353 F. Supp. 900, 927 (D. Ariz. 1972), *aff'd* 512 F.2d 109 (9th Cir. 1975).

[112] G. Gunther, CONSTITUTIONAL LAW 1156 (11th ed. 1985)

[113] 607 S.W.2d 638, 642-43 (Tex. Civ. App. Ct. 1980), *see also* Morrison v. State Bd., 461 P.2d 375 (Cal. 1969) and Hale v. Board of Educ., 234 N.E.2d 583 (Ohio 1968).

proof of dishonesty, "there [also] was proof that the administration of the insurance program was not a professional responsibility of a member of the teaching staff of the University." Texas' Appellate Court affirmed a lower court order requiring reinstatement of the tenured faculty member, stating:

> An agency [University] is not empowered to dismiss an employee whose personal or private conduct incurred the agency's displeasure. Rather, courts consistently relate such terms as "moral turpitude" to the issue of whether the employee's conduct has disqualified him, when applied to the performance of the employee in his particular type of job. . . . In the teaching profession, the inquiry becomes one of whether the teacher's private conduct bears a direct relationship to his ability to teach. In different terms, what is the likelihood that the employee's conduct many have adversely affected students or fellow teachers.

Dismissal grounds such as "moral turpitude," or "uncooperativeness," or "improper professional attitude," etc. seem equally vulnerable to due process of law challenges of vagueness or lack of relatedness, because such bare grounds, by themselves, neither tie the dismissal ground to professional capacities, nor convey sufficient information to qualify as "adequate notice" required by due process of law.

The application of the law of vagueness to an academic context, and specifically to grounds for dismissal of faculty members is in its infancy. It has a long history in constitutional law, but because of judicial deference to decisions of institutions of higher education, it has not yet played a significant role. However, the winds of change are blowing, and timidly but surely courts are beginning to take vagueness arguments seriously.

The University of Alabama dismissed a tenured professor on charges of "insubordination and dereliction of duty" which had been brought pursuant to a tenure code provision permitting dismissal for "adequate cause" as it may be found at a hearing. The faculty member argued in court that the bare "adequate cause" standard, standing alone, was so vague it violated due process of law requirements. Then-recent precedents showed vagueness to be an argument to be taken seriously,[114] but the court, in *Garrett v. Mathews*[115] rejected the vagueness argument in one conclusory sentence, containing no analysis and relying on a previous case that did not even

---

[114] In Tuma v. Board of Nursing, 593 P.2d 711 (Idaho 1979), the court invalidated as vague a suspension under the standard "unprofessional conduct," and in Davis v. Williams, 598 F.2d 916 (5th Cir. 1979), the court invalidated as vague a regulation prohibiting "conduct prejudicial to good order."

[115] 625 F.2d 658 (5th Cir. 1980).

address the vagueness argument.[116] *Garrett* is a precedent in the Fifth Judicial Circuit for the proposition that a bare "adequate cause" standard is constitutional, but it is a limited precedent because of its lack of citation to relevant precedential authority.

The University of Nevada (Reno) dismissed a tenured faculty member alleging that he violated a university code provision requiring him "to exercise appropriate restraint [and] to show respect for the opinions of others" and that the Board of Regents had decided this provision constituted "adequate cause for dismissal." In *Adamian v. Jacobsen*,[117] the faculty member who allegedly had led a disruptive demonstration on campus, argued that the two code requirements were so vague that persons of ordinary intelligence must guess at their specific meanings, and also that they also were overbroad in violation of the First Amendment because they included as dismissal grounds expression protected by the constitution. The court seriously considered the argument, ruling that the standards would be vague and overbroad, and would violate the First Amendment if interpreted broadly, but that they would not be vague and overbroad if interpreted narrowly in conformity with AAUP's *Academic Freedom Guidelines*, which were seen as expressions of special but common understandings and practices of professional academic life, and which would reflect a limitation on the *manner,* not *content,* of the expression. The court later exercised deference to administrative decisionmaking, interpreting the charges narrowly in light of the AAUP Guidelines, and upheld the dismissal. The charges were neither vague nor overbroad when measured by common academic understandings and practices, as evidenced by the AAUP Guidelines.

In *Korf v. Ball State University*,[118] the University had adopted the AAUP's *Statement on Professional Ethics* which was never intended to serve as a statement of specific grounds — "adequate cause" — for dismissal, but was intended as professional guidelines. The Statement prohibits, but does not define, "exploitation of students . . . for private advantage," and requires a professor to demonstrate "respect for the student as an individual and adhere to his proper role as intellectual guide and counselor.[119]" The University dismissed a tenured faculty member for violating these two guidelines, treating them as standards, after a hearing committee found that he had made sexual advances toward, and had exploited, male students. The faculty member sued, claiming vagueness; i.e., the standards violated due process. He claimed they made no reference whatsoever to any aspect of

---

116 Bowling v. Scott, 587 F.2d 229 (5th Cir. 1979).

117 523 F.2d 929 (9th Cir. 1975).

118 726 F.2d 1222 (7th Cir. 1984)

119 AMERICAN ASS'N OF UNIV. PROFESSORS, POLICY REPORTS 75-6 (Washington, D.C. 1990).

sexual conduct, and that therefore, they could not have provided him with adequate notice of the standard to which he actually had been held. The court seriously considered the argument, but exercising deference, it held the charges not to be vague:

> It is unreasonable to assume that the drafters of the "Statement On Professional Ethics" could and must specifically delineate each and every type of conduct (including deviant conduct) constituting a violation . . . We agree with [the faculty member's] academic peers on the hearing committee and the board of trustees . . . [who] were well qualified to interpret the AAUP Statement . . . as well as to determine what is and is not acceptable faculty conduct within an academic setting . . . The facts and circumstances clearly demonstrate that [the faculty member] should have understood both the standards to which he was being held and the consequences of his conduct.

The court accepted a faculty member's vagueness and overbreadth claims in *Bishop v. Aronov*.[120] Bishop, the faculty member, was the Director of the Human Performance Laboratory. He taught exercise physiology to graduates and undergraduates, and supervised research problems and theses at the University of Alabama. He occasionally referred to his personal religious beliefs during instructional time, remarks which he prefaced as personal "bias." Some references concerned his understanding of the creative force behind human physiology and others concerned the foundations of his approach to problems and his advice to students on how he coped with stress (based on the belief that his religious beliefs are more important to him than academic production). He organized an after-class meeting for his students and all other interested persons, and lectured on "Evidences of God in Human Physiology." Some students complained. After several meetings of administrators, Bishop was strictly instructed generally to refrain from interjecting his religious beliefs into instructional time periods and into the optional classes for his students and all other interested persons. Bishop twice sought, and failed, to have the order rescinded, and he sued. Bishop argued that the restriction "rather than being specifically tailored, is vague and over broad." The court agreed:

> The Court holds the University restriction which limits all expression of personal religious views as "unwarranted" is vague and overbroad. It reaches statements not violative of the Establishment Clause and fails to provide adequate

---

120 732 F. Supp. 1562 (N.D. Ala. 1990).

notice of the proscribed speech. The state's interest in
disestablishment cannot overcome federal free speech rights.

Despite the summary approval of a bare "adequate cause" standard in the
Garrett case, other cases make clear that the courts are willing to consider
vagueness (and overbreadth) arguments in an academic dismissal context.
Charges will be reviewed in light of the common understandings and
practices of professionalism in institutional and academic life to determine
whether they provide sufficient due process notice. This trend suggests that
colleges and universities should be sure to include in their tenure codes
specific and clear definitions of the grounds for dismissal, relating them,
directly and substantially, to the fitness of faculty members in their professional capacities as teachers or researchers, thereby providing a sufficiently
clear guide to those who must apply the concepts and forewarning faculty
members who are subject to them.

b. The Hearing

The law historically and the Supreme Court traditionally have placed
enormous weight on the *neutrality* of the entire due process hearing, and
especially on the *neutrality* of the hearing tribunal.[121] Thus, "the right to an
impartial decision-maker is required by due process" in every case.[122]
Because "the appearance of evenhanded justice . . . is at the core of due
process,"[123] courts *may* disqualify decisionmakers who in fact "have no
actual bias" if they reasonably *appear* to be biased.[124] The Supreme Court
has consistently ruled that procedural due process prohibits decisionmakers
from deciding cases whose outcome will directly and substantially affect
their personal financial interests[125] or that of organizations for which they
are personally responsible.[126] Obviously, due process is violated where

---

[121] *Cf.* Dr. Bonham's Case, 8 Co. 114a, 118a (1610) (a "person cannot be judge in his own cause
. . . and one cannot be judge and attorney for any of the parties").

[122] Arnett v. Kennedy, 416 U.S. 134, 197 (1974) (White, J., concurring and dissenting in part).

[123] Mayberry v. Pennsylvania, 400 U.S. 455, 469 (1971) (Harlan, J. concurring).

[124] *See, e.g.*, Morrissey v. Brewer, 408 U.S. 471, 485-86 (1972), but see Kirp, *Proceduralism And
Bureaucracy: Due Process In The School Setting*, 28 STAN. L. REV. 841, 863 (1976) and *compare*,
Megill v. Board of Regents, 541 F.2d 1073, 1079 (5th Cir. 1976) ("The record must support actual
[not merely apparent] partiality of the body or its individual members").

[125] *See, e.g.*, Tumey v. Ohio, 273 U.S. 510 (1927) (judge's salary came from court costs assessed
against *convicted* defendants), and Gibson v. Berryhill, 411 U.S. 564 (1973) (Board of Optometry
composed solely of optometrists in private practice having substantial pecuniary interest in cases
before them should not judge whether to revoke licenses of their competitors; namely "all
optometrists in the State who were employed by business corporations").

[126] *See*, Ward v. Monroeville, 409 U.S. 57 (1972).

decisionmakers "give vent to personal spleen or respond to a personal grievance" in reaching a decision.[127]

In a tenured-faculty dismissal context the Fifth Circuit Court of Appeals has stated the usual rule, holding that due process requires "a hearing before a tribunal that possesses some academic expertise and an apparent impartiality toward the charges."[128] Thus, a tenured faculty member's request that the president of an institution "recuse himself from participation in the hearing due to partiality" cannot be summarily dismissed, but it must be heard, and granted if the claim of partiality is "supported by substantial evidence."[129]

The identification and separation of adversarial and adjudicative functions of a tribunal is critical, but also more difficult where the process is more administrative than formally adjudicative. With respect to adversarial non-criminal proceedings, such as most tenured faculty dismissal hearings, the Supreme Court has required only "that the hearing be conducted by some person other than one initially dealing with the case" because the "officer directly involved in making recommendations cannot always have complete objectivity in evaluating them."[130] Because the President and/or the governing board first must review the evidence as well as the charges, and must conclude that the charges are valid, thereby approving the charges before they are brought, and because they are "the charging authority," the initial hearing in a case should not involve them, but should be conducted before a Tenure Hearing Committee or other body which may include the faculty member's non-administrative academic peers.

In *State v. McPhee*,[131] Dr. Ball, a tenured faculty member, was charged with "inefficiency, failure to cooperate with administrators, conduct unbecoming a teacher and breach of professional ethics, and incompatibility with state laws, board policies and professional environment." At the one-day public hearing held by the Board, its vice president, "who is an attorney," presided over the hearing. "Not only did he preside over the hearing but he also assumed the dual role of acting as counsel for the prosecution in presenting evidence and entering objection to evidence offered in behalf of Dr. Ball," even though the board's legal advisor, an assistant attorney general, was present throughout and could have acted as the prosecutor. Subsequently, the Board met, and by vote of 9 to 1 voted to dismiss Dr. Ball, who appealed to a state court. The court ruled on the above facts, concluding that the Board "had acted arbitrarily and that Dr. Ball had not been accorded

---

[127] Offutt v. United States, 348 U.S. 11, 14 (1954).

[128] Levitt v. University of Tex. El Paso, 759 F.2d 1224, 1228 (5th Cir. 1985), relying on Ferguson v. Thomas, 430 F.2d 852, 856 (5th Cir. 1970).

[129] Cherry v. Bronson, 384 So. 2d 169, 170 (Fla. Dist. Ct. App. 1980).

[130] Morrissey v. Brewer, 408 U.S. 471, 485-86 (1972).

[131] 94 N.W.2d 711 (Wis. 1959).

a fair hearing." The Board appealed. The State Supreme Court affirmed, stating that "the same person should not be put in the position of acting as both attorney and judge" because "when he lays down his duties as advocate and assumes those of judge, his activities in the former capacity may tend to influence his judgment while acting in the latter capacity."

An obvious extension of this principle occurred in *Board of Education v. Lockhart*,[132] where a tenured high school psychology teacher was dismissed for "incompetency, neglect of duty, insubordination, and other good and just cause," because of his refusal to perform mandatory hall supervision at the school due to his belief that such action on his part would contradict "his classroom teaching that students are responsible for their own behavior." William Malone, the school's attorney, "prosecuted the matter for the school district at the evidentiary hearing" before an independent hearing officer who made finding of facts and a recommendation which in turn came before the Board for review. At the Board's review hearing after a motion had been made ordering Lockhart's dismissal, a School Board member directly asked Malone for his recommendation on the matter, Lockhart's attorney objected as going beyond the proper scope of the governing board review. Then another Board member asked: "Bill, does your recommendation [to dismiss] still stand?" Answer: "Yes, it does," immediately upon which the Board voted unanimously to dismiss. The Colorado Supreme Court's reasoning was based on due process analyses, but it ultimately based its decision on the state's Administrative Procedure Act, ruling that the "dismissal was invalid due to unfair procedures employed by the board during its deliberative session; . . . a school board's attorney, who has taken part in the adversary proceedings in the role of prosecutor . . . should take no part in the final deliberations of the board . . . ."

When a governing Board acts as the appellate tribunal and reviews the initial decision of a hearing panel, it must conduct a *good faith* review. "The board must consider all information available from the hearing," and if a record exists it "*must* be considered";[133] however, if "the content of the record is available to the Board through staff [briefings], Board members or counsel, and is considered, due process is satisfied."[134] But, the "failure of [a] Board to, in essence, look beyond the recommendations of its administrators and the brief of its own attorney offends the basic concept of fundamental fairness and deprives [a tenured faculty member] of property without due process of law under the Fourteenth Amendment."[135]

---

[132] Board of Educ. v. Lockhart, 687 P.2d 1306 (Colo. 1984). *See also*, Weissman v. Board of Educ., 547 P.2d 1267 (Colo. 1976) and deKoevand v. Board of Educ., 688 P.2d 219 (Colo. 1984).

[133] Unruh v. Board of Educ., 775 P.2d 171, 174 (Kan. 1989), *but compare*, Bates v. Sponberg, 547 F.2d 325 (6th Cir. 1976).

[134] Kelly v. Kansas City Community College, 648 P.2d 225 (Kan. 1982).

[135] Unruh v. Board of Educ., 775 P.2d 171, 176 (Kan. 1989).

Several recent cases illustrate the Supreme Court's growing tolerance of potential structural institutional biases in non-adjudicatory settings which, may be distinguished from settings involving tenured faculty dismissal adjudications. The Court's attitude is important. Does it apply to Presidential or governing board review of a hearing panel's decision when certain kinds of claims of bias are levelled against the President or Board? The obviously important claim is that a denial of due process occurs when the President or Board first reviews the evidence and the charges, and approves them as valid, and then later, seeks to review them again as part of the formal review of the hearing panel's decision to see whether the charges have been validated by the evidence. *Hortonville School District v. Hortonville Education Association*[136] is a labor law case. The sole issue was "whether the Due Process Clause of the Fourteenth Amendment prohibits this School Board from making the decision to dismiss teachers admittedly engaged in [an illegal] strike and persistently refusing to return to their duties." The Court rejected the teachers' argument that the School Board was necessarily biased because it had been deeply involved in the collective bargaining negotiations with the teachers which proved unsuccessful and which preceded their illegal strike. The Court ruled that the teachers "have failed to demonstrate that the decision to terminate their employment was infected with the sort of bias that we have held to disqualify other decisionmakers as a matter of federal due process," thereby dismissing the teachers' due process challenge to the Board's dismissal decision.

The Supreme Court has generally found that the fundamental right to a hearing consonant with procedural due process embraces at least two broadly conceived rights: (1) the right to present evidence[137] and (2) the right to confront and effectively cross-examine adverse witnesses.[138] All courts agree that in an academic context a tenured faculty member facing dismissal has a due process right to present evidence in his or her favor at the administrative hearing, and it will not be discussed further.[139]

---

[136] 426 U.S. 482 (1976). *See also*, Withrow v. Larkin, 421 U.S. 35, 47, 54-55 (1975); Marshall v. Jerrico, Inc., 446 U.S. 238 (1980), and Schweiker v. McClure, 456 U.S. 188 (1982). *Note also*, Chrysler Corp. v. Texas Motor Vehicle Comm., 755 F.2d 1192, 1199 (5th Cir. 1985).

[137] Morgan v. United States, 304 U.S. 1, 18 (1938).

[138] Green v. McElroy, 360 U.S. 474, 497 (1959).

[139] This requirement is formulated in various ways; for example, in Stewart v. Bailey, 556 F.2d 281, 285 (5th Cir. 1977), after ruling that minimal due process for a tenured faculty member requires (1) notice "in sufficient detail to fairly enable him to show any error that may exist," and (2) advice of "names and nature of the testimony of witnesses against him," the court continued stating that at "a reasonable time after such advice, he must be accorded a meaningful opportunity to be heard in his own defense."

Although the Supreme Court has expressed the view that the "right to be heard would be, in many cases, of little avail if it did not comprehend the right to be heard by counsel,"[140] and has firmly established that right in criminal cases, the Court has pursued a flexible, case-by-case approach in non-criminal cases. In the latter instance, lower courts are not fully agreed on whether the right to be heard includes the right to confront and effectively to cross-examine adverse witnesses through one's lawyer. However, most courts rule in favor of the rights of a faculty member to confront and to cross-examine his or her accusers. For example, in *Haddock v. Board of Education*,[141] the court's ruling included a right to discovery of evidence as well as rights to confrontation and cross-examination, holding that the tenured teacher "had no opportunity to hear the evidence gathered during the independent investigations or to cross-examine the secret witnesses to test their credibility," and that "this procedure was fundamentally unfair . . . and violated Mr. Haddock's right to due process."

In *Frumkin v. Board of Trustees, Kent State*,[142] the court bowed to institutional deference. A tenured professor was subjected to dismissal on the charges of "unsatisfactory performance as grant director, unproven charges against faculty members, unprofessional conduct, false charges against the department, and violation of university policy." He was permitted to produce evidence in his favor and to have his lawyer at the hearing, but the lawyer's role was limited to advising his client and making a closing argument on his client's behalf; the lawyer could not conduct any direct or cross-examination of witnesses or raise objections. "Because universities have traditionally been afforded broad discretion in their administration of internal affairs," the court ruled that it did "not deem it necessary to interfere where, as here, there is no showing that the overall procedure was prejudicial to the rights [of the] terminated employee." Presumably, on this reasoning in the *Frumkin* case, the university need not have permitted the faculty member to have his lawyer present at the hearing at all. Several lower courts have found adequate grounds justifying a due-process requirement that an institution honor rights of confrontation and effective cross-examination by a lawyer in administrative hearings, while other courts in cases like *Frumkin*, have denied such rights, believing that the overall process followed in the hearing was fundamentally fair.

Although all courts do not require that the initial hearing panel make formal written findings of fact and conclusions of law at the end of a hearing, they do require the panel adequately to state in writing the reasons for its

---

[140] Goldberg v. Kelly, 397 U.S. 254, 268-69 (1970), (quoting Powell v. Alabama, 287 U.S. 45 at 68-69 (1932)).

[141] 661 P.2d 368 (Kan. 1983).

[142] 626 F.2d 19, 21-22 (6th Cir. 1980).

determination and to identify the specific evidence it relied on, distinguishing that evidence from the remainder.[143] If the record of the hearing panel does not reveal the evidence and the facts found to be determinative, and does not reveal the reasoning behind the decision, then there can be no assurance that the due-process requirement of a reasoned decision on the evidence has been met, and governing boards, and later courts on review, are severely hampered. Furthermore, if the initial hearing panel (1) fails to make adequate findings to support its decision, and (2) fails to identify its reasoning, then that lack places the appellant in an untenable position, infringing on the due-process right of the faculty member or the institution to prepare, present and to receive an effective appellate review of the panel's action. It is suggested these panels make a verbatim transcript of all of the evidence presented, and they write clear and succinct opinions carefully identifying from the corpus of evidence submitted the facts relied upon for decision, and also set forth fully the reasons believed to justify the panel's conclusion.

3. Recommended Guidelines for Procedures

Courts have not laid down a strict set of procedures — a "due process checklist" — required by due process of law in dismissal cases involving tenured faculty members. Instead, they proceed on a case-by-case basis. Yet, certain basics, as identified above, are required by courts. Courts will continue to review the entire process on a case-by-case basis to identify whether fundamental fairness has occurred. This situation creates an opportunity for institutions of higher education to devise procedures in their tenure codes that will resolve doubts, insuring fundamental fairness, and thereby insulating institutional decisions from being reversed by courts for failure to provide adequate due process of law.[144]

The procedural dimensions of due process required two basic elements: adequately specific notice and some kind of a neutral, fair and effective hearing. The precedents reviewed above indicate that when insisting on specific procedures courts have been faithful to the flexibility found in the concept of tenure, and have implemented that concept with procedural requirements which are, themselves, flexible, varying with the perceived needs of a case, and which are quite sensitive to institutions of higher education remaining fully capable of achieving all of their educational goals. Moreover, the procedures necessitated by the due-process-of-law require-

---

[143] *See, e.g.*, Clark v. West Virginia Bd. of Regents, 279 S.E.2d 169 (W. Va. 1981).
[144] Guidelines were suggested by AAUP in its 1982 Recommended Institutional Regulations on Academic Freedom and Tenure (see Appendix to this Study)

ments, illustrated by the cases discussed in this section, in no way preclude, or unwarrantedly hinder, any institution from removing a tenured faculty member because of demonstrated professional incompetence or dishonesty or for manifest and substantial neglect of duty, including insubordination. To the contrary, the legally required procedures actually aid institutions by insuring accuracy, fairness and simple justice when making dismissal decisions.

G. Judicial Review of Institutional Decisions Dismissing Tenured Faculty Members for Cause

A 1971 survey of eighty colleges and universities discovered that only about half of them provided specific grounds for dismissal of tenured faculty for cause beyond the bare statement of "adequate cause" or merely, "cause." The other half of the institutions reported an array of some twenty-five different grounds used for termination.[145] Despite the variety and abstract generality of the standards actually used for dismissal of tenured faculty members (some version of incompetency, insubordination, immorality, unethical conduct and medical disability are the most common grounds in dismissal cases), analytically the cases boil down to involving one or more of the three grounds set forth in the title of this section. This study organizes its comments around these three grounds.

In the absence of a claim of deprivation of a substantive or procedural right, court review of an institution's decision to dismiss a tenured faculty member is limited. Courts give large amounts of deference to personnel decisions by institutional administrators by applying the "substantial evidence" rule to them (discussed *supra*). The deference given by courts is especially strong when institutional dismissal decisions *solely* involve professional qualification questions, such as whether a faculty member is professionally competent, or professionally responsible, or whether a faculty

---

[145] B. Shaw, ACADEMIC TENURE IN AMERICAN HIGHER EDUCATION, 62-65 (1971). Court pronouncements frequently do nothing to alleviate problems of vagueness and the lack of relationship of the ground to professional competence and responsibility. For example, a state court has "explained" the good cause standard stating that: "Good cause includes any ground which is put forward by the [Board] in good faith and which is not arbitrary, irrational, unreasonable, or irrelevant to the [Board's] task of building up and maintaining an efficient school system." Harris v. Board of Trustees of State Colleges, 542 N.E.2d 261, 268 (Mass 1989), (quoting Rinaldo v. School Comm., 1 N.E.2d 37 (Mass. 1936)). *Also see*, Lovain, *Grounds For Dismissing Tenured Post Secondary Faculty For Cause*, 10 J. OF COLL. & UNIV. LAW 419 (1983-84).

member's teaching or research meets professionally acceptable standards for promotion, for an award of tenure or for the removal of tenure:[146]

> A teacher's competence and qualifications for tenure or promotion are by their very nature matters calling for highly subjective determinations, determinations which do not lend themselves to precise qualifications and are not susceptible to mechanical measurement or the use of standardized tests. The determinations are in "an area in which school officials must remain free to exercise their judgment" especially since these determinations present unique questions for judgment by those with expertise in the specialized academic area, capable of making professional evaluations of those elusive and intangible qualities and talents expected of the scholar and teacher. Courts are not qualified to review and substitute their judgments for these subjective, discretionary judgments of professional experts on faculty promotions or to engage independently in an intelligent informal comparison of the scholarly contributions or teaching talents of one faculty member denied promotion [or tenure] with those of another faculty member granted a promotion [or tenure]; in short courts may not engage in "second guessing" the University authorities in connection with faculty promotions [tenure awards or tenure removals].

1. Incompetence or Dishonesty In Teaching or Research (Including Inefficiency)

Bevli v. Brisco[147] appears to be a case that could have been avoided if the institution had practiced a "strict" — a severe up-or-out — system of tenure. Charged essentially with demonstrated professional incompetence,

---

[146] Clark v. Whiting, 607 F.2d 634, 639-40 (4th Cir. 1979). ("Denial of a faculty promotion based on an evaluation of the faculty member's 'scholarly achievements' is exactly the type of determination which . . . is not justiciable in federal court . . . . [a]nd that has long been the ruling uniformly applied by the courts . . ."). *Also see* Lewis v. Chicago State College, 299 F. Supp 1357, 1359-60 (N.D. Ill. 1969) ("The judiciary is not the appropriate forum for decisions involving academic rank. A professor's value depends upon his creativity, his rapport with students and colleagues, his teaching ability, and numerous other intangible qualities which cannot be measured by objective standards").

[147] 212 Cal. Rptr 36 (Cal. Ct. App. 1985).

the faculty member, a chemistry teacher with 15 years service, first argued that she had not received a fair hearing, which the court rejected:[148]

> It appears to this court that requesting [the faculty member] to perform experiments which she had been responsible for teaching over a number of years would hardly constitute unfairness, particularly when the experiments were the subject of the complaints which gave rise to these proceedings.

The initial decisionmaker (a mutually agreed upon arbitrator) found (and the appellate court approvingly reported) that the institution had proved its charge of "unfitness for service," specifically noting that she was unable "to define certain words, explain basic concepts of chemistry such as 'significant numbers,' the amount of electrical power going through a system, the Dumas method of determining molecular weight, conduct an electrolysis experiment, or radiation experiment although supplied with the necessary equipment," eventually concluding that "she is unable to employ knowledge of the subject matter at a professional level."

In *Chung v. Park*,[149] a tenured professor of biology at Mansfield State College was dismissed after five years of service "for incompetence and intransigence with respect to his dealings with his superiors."[150] President Park's letter of notification suggested that the faculty member failed to communicate effectively and stated that "there was significant concern among students about the quality of Dr. Chung's teaching"; that the "department could not assign him his full share of teaching responsibilities," and that "Dr. Chung had refused to cooperate with the department and his colleagues in efforts to identify and resolve the above problems."[151] The hearing committee found "that the evidence clearly supported the conclusion that the reasons stated in the President's letter had factual bases . . . ." Dr. Chung obtained federal court review, which ruled "that the hearing provided Dr. Chung fully satisfied the college's tenure regulations and the requirements of due process."

In *King v. University of Minnesota*[152] a black, tenured, full professor in the Department of Afro-American Studies was dismissed on charges that amounted to demonstrated professional incompetency and substantial and manifest neglect of duty, which were upheld by the court. There were

---

[148] The court also ruled that the institution is entitled to plead multiple causes for dismissal which are all or in part supported by common factual allegations, stating that "this court is unaware of any rule of law which proscribes the use of single facts to support multiple theories of legal responsibility." *Id*. at 38.

[149] 514 F.2d 382 (3d Cir. 1975).

[150] Chung v. Park, 377 F. Supp. 524, 529 (M.D. Pa. 1974).

[151] Chung v. Park, 514 F.2d 382, 384 (3d Cir. 1975).

[152] 774 F.2d 224 (8th Cir. 1985), this case is partially described in note 52, *supra*.

"complaints about King's performance by students, by colleagues, and by the successive chairmen of the Department." The specific "complaints concerned poor teaching performance, excessive unexcused absences from class, absences from faculty meetings, undocumented research, and other matters." The hearing committee "recommended that King be terminated for cause under the Tenure Code," which ultimately occurred. The court affirmed, summarily rejecting King's claims that he had been subjected to racial discrimination, and had not received procedural due process, specifically noting that the notice King had received was complete, definite and specific; that the hearing panel consisted of King's academic peers and one member was replaced after King's objection; that "a pre-hearing conference was held at which the parties exchanged issue lists, witness lists and exhibit lists;" that the tribunal issued a pre-hearing order identifying the issues to be tried, and entertained and ruled on objections to its order; that King was represented by a lawyer throughout who presented oral and documentary evidence in King's behalf, cross-examined witnesses and made oral and written arguments to the tribunal and that King "was allowed substantial document discovery." The University's procedures can be seen as a useful model of due process. Apart from showing that incompetent professors with tenure can be dismissed, this case also shows that if a University honestly administers a tenure code affording full due process of law, it need have no qualms about being taken to court.

Agarwal v. Regents of University of Minnesota[153] not only illustrates that a tenured faculty member can be dismissed for demonstrated professional incompetence and dishonesty, but also provides insight into the kinds of supporting evidence a court will find acceptable. A tenured associate professor of physics was dismissed on charges of demonstrated professional incompetence and plagiarism "in the preparation of three physics laboratory manuals for use in introductory courses on the Morris campus of the University," for which he had been reprimanded and denied merit salary increase for one year. Thereafter, eight physics majors, all former students of his, filed a formal grievance against Agarwal complaining that "he had displayed a lack of moral integrity in the plagiarism incident and in his unauthorized examination of confidential documents concerning another professor, and that he was incompetent as a teacher, frequently harassing students and behaving in an unprofessional manner toward colleagues." These charges were found proven by a five-member faculty committee, after which Agarwal was formally charged with demonstrated professional incompetence and plagiarism. These charges were heard by a hearing committee. It ruled against Agarwal on both counts, and he was dismissed.

---

[153] 788 F.2d 504 (8th Cir. 1986).

He sued in a federal court, and lost, with the court ruling "that a court's role is limited to examining the record of University proceedings to determine whether there was substantial evidence to support its determination" and "that substantial evidence in the form of the student's testimony concerning Agarwal's classroom conduct, the opinions offered by his colleagues concerning the competence of a professor who would engage in such conduct, and the results of student evaluation surveys, supported the decision to terminate Agarwal's employment."

In *Jawa v. Fayetteville State University*[154] a tenured professor in the Department of Education and Psychology was dismissed essentially for demonstrated professional incompetence and irresponsibility and for substantial and manifest neglect of duties. Jawa claimed his dismissal and other grievances were "all because of his race and national origin," which the court rejected. It expressly stated that:

> This court finds as a fact that plaintiff [Jawa] was a poor teacher who was apparently unwilling to prepare for class; that he had difficulty interacting with students and had little interest in his students; that he failed to keep office hours and to advise properly his students; that he was uncooperative with his colleagues and the administration; that he was unwilling or unable to follow the appropriate and proper directives of his superiors and comply with University policies and procedures; and that plaintiff's reckless disregard for the truth resulted in accusing his superiors of incompetence and discriminatory practices against him.

The Supreme Judicial Court of Massachusetts recently sustained an institution's decision to dismiss a tenured professor of physics essentially on grounds of professional irresponsibility (or was it really because the faculty member was an unmitigated nuisance?). The formal ground was that the faculty member "had engaged in personal conduct which impaired his ability to fulfill his institutional responsibilities and thus related to his professional fitness."[155] After noting that "it is not for this court to rule on the wisdom of tenure policy for State educational institutions" and "that the decision of the board of trustees will be upheld unless each of the stated reasons for termination is trivial, or is unrelated to the educational process or to working relationships within the educational institution," the court turned to the case at hand and admitted that some of the charges "viewed in isolation, may not support a finding of just cause for dismissal." Nevertheless, the faculty

---

[154] 426 F. Supp. 218 (E.D.N.C. 1976).
[155] Harris v. Board of Trustees of State Colleges, 542 N.E.2d 261, 268 (Mass. 1989).

member had "engaged in a pattern which, when viewed as a whole, supported a conclusion that he was unfit to remain a tenured faculty member." The court cited the following facts in justification:

> There was evidence, among other things, that the [faculty member] repeatedly belittled his students, falsely stated that he had applied for a permit to carry a gun to protect himself against a squirt-gun toting student and constantly harassed his fellow faculty members, administrators, and support staff. We conclude that the board acted within its discretionary authority . . .

In *Barszcz v. Board of Trustees*,[156] the court sustained a dismissal for professional dishonesty; the faculty member had misrepresented his academic credentials. He claimed at the time of hiring that he would be awarded a master's degree within several months, which was not forthcoming. Three years later he was awarded tenure, and wore a master's robe to graduation ceremonies. He was dismissed after the truth was discovered.

In *Community College v. McKinley*,[157] a radiology instructor took two additional *part-time* jobs — one at a hospital and one at a funeral home — and was charged with violating a Board policy prohibiting *full-time* outside employment by *full-time* faculty members and with dishonesty; i.e., "false and intentional misrepresentations of outside employment." There was evidence indicating "that McKinley had been hired as a part-time employee . . . . [but] had received full-time benefits merely as an employment inducement because he was a high caliber employee." A hearing officer found dishonesty: "that McKinley had falsified his outside employment disclosure statements but concluded that discharge was too harsh a punishment," disproportionate for that amount of dishonesty. The Board appealed, but the court ruled "that the findings and conclusions of the hearing officer were neither arbitrary nor unreasonable."

Some institutions dismiss faculty members on grounds of "inefficiency." In *Saunders v. Reorganized School District*,[158] Missouri's Supreme Court sustained the dismissal of a tenured, community college faculty member on charges of "inefficiency" and "insubordination," ruling that they were supported by substantial evidence relating to the faculty member's manner of teaching class. The court found that the School Board's findings were supported by "substantial evidence" that:

> Saunders had failed and refused to instruct the curriculum as requested; that he refused to discuss the curriculum

---

[156] 400 F. Supp. 675 (N.D. Ill. 1975).
[157] 513 N.E.2d 951 (Ill. App. Ct. 1987).
[158] 520 S.W.2d 29 (Mo. 1975).

> and its teaching with his superiors; that he gave one second-
> year class a choice as to whether he should teach the first
> year material again or "teach the subject matter as he
> wanted to"; that he refused to participate in the preparation
> of the course outline; that he refused to discuss teacher
> evaluations with his superiors; that he had been inefficient
> as shown by the evaluation reports; that he refused and
> failed to use the required textbooks in his teaching . . . that
> he had been guilty of excessive and unreasonable absence
> . . . .

"Inefficiency" was ruled unproven by courts in two cases that also contained considerable evidence showing that the charge of "inefficiency" was pretextual and weak at best. However, when evidence of professional incompetence is supported by substantial evidence, especially in teaching and research, courts will defer to the legally presumed expertise of academic administrators and governing boards, even in cases having unproven but strong pretextual overtones. In the first case,[159] a California court rejected a charge of "inefficiency" against Dr. Walker, a resident psychiatrist at U.C.L.A. The charge might also be seen as a pretext for an attack on his academic freedom. Dr. Walker was alleged to be "inefficient" because "the central theme that interferes with your work and which is stubbornly unchangeable . . . is your underlying and unremitting belief that missed organic and structural brain changes are the cause of psychological distress and are the proper focus for intervention. . . . It is this one-sidedness that makes your performance . . . inadequate and unacceptable." Dr. Walker "would consider the possibility of an organic basis for mental illness in 30 to 40 per cent of his cases." Thus, the charge of inefficiency came down to the fact that Dr. Walker "had not given 'reasonable attention to the appropriate dynamic factors,'" then much favored at U.C.L.A., because he also insisted on too frequently considering "organic" factors. The court stated that it was "intolerable that Dr. Walker's dismissal should be upheld because his views failed to conform to current theoretical dogma on the causes of mental illness," and concluded by ruling "that the record contains no substantial evidence to support the Board's finding that Dr. Walker was inefficient . . . ."

In the second case, *State v. McPhee*,[160] a tenured faculty member was dismissed on charges of a lack of "efficiency and good behavior," which were ruled unproven. The charges and the evidence offered in their support

---

[159] Walker v. State Personnel Bd., 94 Cal. Rptr. 132 (Cal. 1971).
[160] 94 N.W.2d 711 (Wis. 1959).

showed the charges to be insubstantial and also to be an attack on academic freedom. One of the items of evidence offered in support of the charges was that the faulty member "attempted to persuade graduates not to accept northern Wisconsin teaching jobs," to which the court responded: "Even if true, such conduct does not constitute either inefficiency or bad behavior." Another item of evidence showed that the faculty member had attacked graduate programs of the college in which students were allowed to take courses offered as part of the bachelor's degree program, to which the court responded:

> Surely a teacher in a state college is entitled to some academic freedom in criticizing school programs with which he is in disagreement. Such acts of criticism do not qualify as either inefficiency or bad behavior.

Cases can involve both a failure of professional competence and responsibility, and also a substantial and manifest neglect of professional duties. For example, in *Riggin v. Board of Trustees of Ball State University*,[161] the faculty member, in 1981, essentially was found to have violated both. The court's discussion gives insight into the kinds of evidence sufficient to sustain both charges:

> The court's review of the decisions of the committee and the Board of Trustees was not a hearing *de novo*. Rather, its sole function was to determine whether the action was illegal, or arbitrary and capricious. In doing so it must accept the evidence most favorable to support the administrative decision.

> Testimony against Riggin was given by department heads, deans, fellow faculty members and former *cum laude* students. That testimony revealed that problems concerning Riggin's competence surfaced as early as 1977. At that time the dean of his school and the head of his department voiced criticism of Riggin's performance as a teacher and as a faculty member, and they attempted to effect an improvement in his performance. The deficiencies complained of included lack of preparation; showing too many irrelevant films which consumed about one-third of class time; lack of teaching material or aids (justified by Riggin on the grounds that he had taught so long that he did not need them); a reading list which contained no books

---

[161] 489 N.E.2d 616 (Ind. Ct. App. 1986), *transfer den.* 499 N.E.2d 243 (Ind. 1986).

published later than 1968 and that had not been updated since 1975; haphazard lectures; lack of diligence in completing course content; and failure to assign problems in a course, finance, that routinely calls for such.

There was evidence that at least some of his students were not prepared to advance in Riggin's particular area of discipline and that some could not meet minimum qualifications for advanced work. He spent an inordinate amount of class time on non-pertinent matters such as telling stories and talking about his dairy business, athletics, his experiences as a legislator, current events, lawsuits in which he had been involved, and the societal influence of bankers. Some witnesses concluded that he spent 50% to 75% of class time on such irrelevant matters.

There was evidence that he was non-cooperative in the area of teaching assignments and class scheduling, yet demanded schedules, without consideration of departmental needs, which gave him large blocks of time in which to pursue personal endeavors. He even changed class scheduling without departmental approval. In at least one instance he refused to teach a class offered by his department.

There was evidence that Riggin failed to adequately participate in departmental, collegiate and university affairs. He attended only five out of the last sixteen Finance Department meetings, and did not participate in those that he did attend. He did not participate in syllabus or curriculum formulation, or in textbook selection. He had not served on any doctoral committees since the early 1970's, and had not been a member of a university committee for 12 years.

There was evidence that he had not engaged in research or scholarly activities for at least 10 years, had not belonged to any professional organizations, and did not attend any academic organization meetings. At one time he belonged to a number of organizations, but had since dropped out.

There was evidence that research, scholarly activities, attendance at some professional organization meetings, participation in departmental and university affairs, and cooperation with fellow faculty members, department heads, and deans were expected of every faculty member including Riggin. Attempts by his superiors to communicate with him over a course of years met with rebuffs. He was belligerent, threatened to bring law suits and demanded that his attorney be present at conferences. He not only refused to alter his behavior, but refused to discuss it, characterizing the activities of his superiors as a "conspiracy." Riggin's argument here is without basis. It is merely an invitation to reweigh the evidence.

2. Neglect Of Professional Duty (Including Insubordination)

Neglect of duty must be "substantial" and "manifest." To determine whether the neglect of professional duty is "substantial," the focus is on the "*neglect*" of the duty, and not on the duty itself. The neglect must be substantial; that is, the neglect of the duty must be seen as important, weighty, and as the failure to attend to something of considerable real worth in the academic scheme of things. Of course, the importance of the duty is a factor to weigh in the calculus, and a few breaches (or even one) of a very important duty might be considered "substantial;" whereas several breaches of a duty considered trivial or unimportant might not qualify. The dimension of substantial neglect is illustrated by a federal court case in which the judge stated that of "the eight specific deeds which the Board [of Regents at Arizona State University] found plaintiff did and which provide the basis for the Board's finding of unfitness and discharge, only one concerns plaintiff's functions as a teacher, i.e., one unexcused class cancellation; [a]ll of the other charges involve extramural or public activity."[162] The court earlier had found as a fact "that the incident was an isolated one and that plaintiff's record in following university policy in favor of meeting class schedules is otherwise excellent."[163] Thus, from the perspective of this Study, while this case shows that there was some "neglect," it also shows that "neglect" to be marginal and trivial, and it can not be classified as "substantial."

Neglect of duty is "*manifest*" when the "*neglect*" (not the duty, itself) is palpable; that is, when facts reveal the neglect to be so plainly obvious to the

---

[162] Starsky v. Williams, 353 F. Supp. 900, 916-17 (D. Ariz. 1972).

[163] *Id.* at 910. "The evidence is uncontradicted that plaintiff [Professor Starsky] is extremely conscientious about meeting classes, even going to class when he can hardly talk;" that "there was uncontradicted evidence that somewhat casual canceling of classes is not uncommon at Arizona State University," and that "Professor Starsky was not breaking any department rule in canceling the class since there was long standing autonomy in this connection." *Id.* at 909.

eye, mind or judgment that there can be no reasonable doubt about its existence whatsoever.

"*Insubordination*" has been defined as the willful refusal of a teacher to obey the reasonable rules and regulations of the governing board[164] or as disobedience of orders, or direction, with a general disaffected attitude toward authority.[165] "Insubordination may consist of a persistent course of willful defiance in refusing to obey a reasonable direct or implied order given by proper authority."[166] A state appellate court has summarized past cases on insubordination and applied them, saying:[167]

> In those cases where insubordination was charged due to an absence by the teacher and the teacher had notified the proper authorities of the proposed absence and approval of such was expressly denied, the dismissals for insubordination were affirmed . . . .

> Here Professor Stastny's conduct was insubordinate. It was persistent in that even though he received two letters denying approval of his requested absence [to return four days late after Christmas vacation] and directing him to be present and carry out his assigned duties during the winter quarter, he went on his trip as he had planned. His conduct was willful. The final letter warned him that if he ignored the directive, disciplinary measures would be instituted . . . . Notwithstanding this warning, he defied it and went to Israel [to lecture], absenting himself from his duties contrary to the express directive of the university . . . . In light of the extensive absences previously approved by the university, the disapproval in this instance was not unreasonable. The Board's findings support the conclusion Professor Stastny was insubordinate . . . . [His dismissal was upheld by the court.]

Another court has ruled that if the standard is "Gross Insubordination," it had not been met by an "isolated outburst [when the school employee said, "This is what I think of this and you too," wadding up a document and

---

[164] See, Annotation, What Constitutes "Insubordination" As Grounds For Dismissal Of Public School Teacher, 78 A.L.R.3d 83, §§ at 90 (1977).

[165] Coleman v. State, 189 So. 2d 415 (Fla. Dist. Ct. App. 1966) and State v. Board of Regents, 269 P.2d 265 (Nev. 1954).

[166] Board of Trustees v. Colewell, 611 P.2d 427 (Wyo. 1980).

[167] Stastney v. Board of Trustees of Cent. Wash. Univ., 647 P.2d 496, 503 (Wash. Ct. App. 1982).

throwing it on a desk] and could not have been deemed 'constant or continuing'" which is required for the insubordination to qualify as "gross."[168]

The determination of "insubordination" or substantial and manifest *neglect* of professional duty includes consideration of the reasonableness of a faculty member's action, or lack of it, judged against the totality of the facts and circumstances surrounding a case. Professional duties, properly conceived, run both ways; that is, between the institution and faculty members, and not merely one way only from the faculty member to the institution. The view that professional duties, properly conceived, constitute a two-way street was at stake in *McConnell v. Howard University.*[169] A white, tenured associate professor of mathematics taught an algebra class of forty black students, and, on the basis of ten years past experience, he advised the students to cut back on their other commitments, by taking a reduced course load and by limiting their out-of class obligations, so they would have sufficient time to study and prepare for his algebra class. Early in the course, he administered a one-question quiz to the class based on previous materials he had covered, but only five of forty students answered the question correctly. At the next class he repeated his advice about cutting back on commitments, and told the class a fable about a monkey who put his hand into a cookie jar and was unable to get his hand out because he had tried to grab too many cookies and was unwilling to let go of some of them.

Later during the class he asked two students to refrain from talking between themselves; whereupon, one, a female, called him a "condescending, patronizing racist." He demanded she apologize; she refused and he finished the class, and then asked her to meet with him. She refused. He tried to speak with her before the next class session. She refused. He then raised the subject in class, saying she should apologize. She refused and said: "go on and teach the course." Whereupon, he asked her to leave; she refused, and he called the Office for Security. She was privately admonished by the Dean for Special Student Services that any further activity of this kind would result in disciplinary action.

At the next meeting of the class the faculty member renewed his request that she apologize or leave the room; she refused, and he dismissed the class. He was told by the departmental chair that his action could be considered neglect of duty, and he replied he would not return until the University restored to his classroom the right atmosphere of student-teacher relationships and academic freedom conducive to learning. He continued to teach other assigned courses, but refused to teach his algebra class until, in his view, the University discharged its duty. He was dismissed for neglect of duty.

---

[168] Smith v. School Bd., 405 So. 2d 183, 185 (Fla. Dist. Ct. App. 1981).
[169] 818 F.2d 58 (D.C. Cir. 1987).

He sued the private University for breach of contract, and lost in the trial court. He appealed, and won a new trial based, in part, on his theory of the case. The issue, the court of appeals said, was not whether he failed to teach class, but "whether Dr. McConnell's *failure* to teach assigned classes constituted *neglect* of his professional responsibilities." Failure to teach the class, by itself, was NOT the issue, nor did it conclusively demonstrate neglect of duty, nor was it determinative of the case. Neglect of professional duties was the issue:

> We agree with appellant [McConnell]. The term "neglect" necessarily implies an assessment as to whether Dr. McConnell's actions, given the entire factual context, were within the acceptable range of conduct within his profession. The Grievance Committee's findings suggest that Dr. McConnell's action may well not have constituted a neglect of professional responsibilities. [It] stated that, in its view, Dr. McConnell's decision not to teach the class was an attempt "to restore what [he] believed to be standard teacher-student relationships," . . . and that "it is convincingly clear from the evidence presented that his departmental colleagues, including the Departmental Chairman, fail to view him as being professionally negligent." At trial, Dr. McConnell should be allowed to present evidence that, under the facts and circumstances of this case, he acted within the bounds of reasonable behavior for a professor. . . . In short, we believe that the term "neglect of professional responsibilities," by its very words, includes a consideration of the reasonableness of Dr. McConnell's actions under the totality of the circumstances surrounding them.

As discussed above, the employment contracts of faculty members employed by private[170] and public[171] institutions of higher education almost always are interpreted to include the institution's rules and regulations, including its tenure code. In very few, perhaps even questionable, cases having quite unique facts, courts have ruled that a substantial and manifest neglect of certain specific duties by the faculty member constituted a voluntary abandonment and relinquishment of the contract itself, and all of tenure's rights and protections. For example, in *Kalme v. West Virginia State*

---

[170] *See* note 45, *supra*.
[171] *See, e.g.,* Koch v. Board of Trustees, Univ. of Ill., 187 N.E.2d 340 (Ill. App. Ct. 1963).

Board of Regents,[172] the tenured faculty member signed a contract to return after a year's leave of absence and to continue teaching at West Virginia State for academic year 1973-74. He also signed a second contract for the same academic year obligating him to teach at the Interamerican University in Puerto Rico. He failed to appear at West Virginia State to resume teaching and other duties which, in turn, were handled by other faculty members. On the day classes began, the President received a letter from the faculty member requesting extension of his leave of absence to finish his doctorate at University of Ottawa (not mentioning Puerto Rico or the Interamerican University contract). The President responded in a letter, later approved by the Board, stating that the institution "no longer considers you in the employment of West Virginia State College or in an official leave capacity." The faculty member's lawsuit in federal court alleging that West Virginia State had deprived him of a constitutionally protected property interest and had breached its contract, was summarily rejected by the court:

> The State, through the college president and Board of Regents, took no action against Kalme; the government did nothing to him; nor did it seek to deprive him any property or liberty interest. To the contrary, the college was quite willing to have him return and signed a contract to accomplish precisely that. The conduct which led to Kalme's loss of employment and tenure rights was initiated by Kalme himself. The Fourteenth Amendment does not protect citizens against the voluntary, unilateral relinquishment of known rights. Kalme intentionally and flagrantly violated his contract of employment with the college, and it was upon this contractual relationship that any "property interest" depended. By failing to appear for work pursuant to the terms of his agreement, Kalme abandoned his rights under it. . . .

Smith v. Kent State University[173] presents a different kind of case of substantial and manifest neglect of duty which, in this instance, basically was insubordination. A tenured faculty member in the philosophy department he could not "get along." He was transferred to the School of Music, where as coordinator of the Music History and Literature Division, he taught, *inter alia,* a basic course in Music History for which he received an unfavorable student rating in 1970. He also sought to have the Director discharged. After

---

[172] 539 F.2d 1346 (4th Cir. 1976). *Also see* Akyeampong v. Coppin State College, 538 F. Supp. 986 (D. Md. 1982). ("The evidence adduced at trial shows that this case is indistinguishable from Kalme.")

[173] 696 F.2d 477 (6th Cir. 1983).

again being assigned to the course for 1971-72, he wrote the Assistant Director of the School of Music indicating that he would not teach it. The Assistant Director, the Director and the Dean advised the faculty member that he was the logical person to teach the course, but he again was refused. Thereafter, a hearing on dismissal was held, with the Committee recommending against dismissal as too severe a sanction if the faculty member would agree to accept the authority of the Music Director with respect to class assignments, which he said he would, and which the Board made an express condition of his reappointment. Later when told he had been assigned to teach Music History during 1972-73, the faculty member advised that he would not teach the course, and would take the matter up with his lawyer. He did not meet the class for its first session, but later his lawyer assured administrators that the faculty member would teach the course pending resolution of the dispute. "Once again, however, when the class was again scheduled to convene, Smith [the faculty member] failed to appear, and adamantly refused to discuss the matter with a designated faculty representative." The faculty member was terminated, which was upheld by the court:

> Under the facts set out, KSU had just cause to terminate
> Smith regardless of his tenured status, particularly in light
> of his persistent actions not only flouting the authority of
> the Music Department director but also in refusing to meet
> his scheduled classes.

In *Prebble v. Brodrick*,[174] the faculty member's dismissal for substantial and manifest neglect of professional duties (failure to meet class) was upheld by the court. At the hearing the following facts were admitted:

> Prebble [the tenured faculty member] said it seemed
> correct to him that he did not conduct any of his three
> classes on eight different dates or on the regularly sched-
> uled final exam dates. Prebble said some absences oc-
> curred while he was interviewing for a new position and
> some while he was elk hunting. In each instance the
> students were notified in advance and instructed to study
> certain material.

In *Shaw v. Board of Trustees*[175] two faculty members — one tenured and one on a continuing appointment — were dismissed essentially for substantial and manifest neglect of duty and insubordination. They were charged with failing to attend a required faculty workshop and commencement

---

174 535 F.2d 605 (10th Cir. 1975).
175 549 F.2d 929 (4th Cir. 1976).

exercises, which they admitted to having missed in protest of the College's abolition of its tenure system, and for failing to meet a deadline for faculty members to submit an acceptable letter of contrition for their attitude and for missing the workshop and commencement. The court found the institution's decision not to be in retaliation for exercising constitutionally protected rights of expression, and upheld the dismissals. The courts also agreed with the Board in *Garret v. Mathews*[176] that a faculty member's failure to comply with a reasonable administrative request to supply a list of publications and the faculty member's subsequent failure to open his mail from the administration constituted neglect of professional duty and insubordination, justifying dismissal. The faculty member argued that there was no written rule specifically imposing a duty requiring faculty members to open mail or to supply publication lists. The court responded: "Though, as plaintiff alleges, supplying a list of publications and opening mail may be nowhere written as job requirements, the court notes that not showing up for class naked is not a written job requirement either. Some things go without saying."

A tenured faculty member was dismissed, in part, because of neglect of duty for failure to submit required reports on a project he was directing.[177] The dismissal of a tenured professor was upheld in another case. After accepting an assignment to develop guidelines and content of two graduate courses for fall term and after having permission to use three months leave in which to do it all, she "never produced one aspect of the task assigned her, she produced no notes, rough drafts, comments or observations."[178] In another case, the court found valid neglect of duty grounds for dismissing a tenured faculty member because of his repeated failures (1) to keep office hours, (2) to advise his students, and (3) to follow appropriate directives from administrators and comply with institutional policies.[179] In yet another case, dismissals for neglect of duty of two tenured faculty members — one a departmental chair — were upheld because they refused to sign required documents that would limit their outside income from medical practice.[180]

A consideration of the cases found in this section demonstrates that courts have had little difficulty affirming decisions of governing boards that afford appropriate due process procedures and that dismiss faculty members on proven grounds of demonstrated incompetence or dishonesty in professional teaching or research, including inefficiency, or on grounds of substantial and manifest neglect of professional duty, including insubordination. These grounds are believed to be the ones, if any, most likely to be applied

---

[176] 474 F. Supp. 594 (N.D. Ala. 1979), *aff'd*, 625 F.2d 658 (5th Cir. 1980).
[177] Bates v. Sponberg, 547 F.2d 325 (6th Cir. 1976).
[178] Josberger v. University of Tenn., 706 S.W.2d 300, 302 (Tenn. Ct. App. 1985).
[179] Jawa v. Fayetteville State Univ., 426 F. Supp. 218, 224 (E.D.N.C. 1976).
[180] Gross v. University of Tenn., 448 F. Supp. 245 (W.D. Tenn. 1978).

to faculty members aged seventy or over when "uncapping" occurs. It would appear that the legal aspects of tenure constitute no unwarranted, or too costly, or insurmountable, barrier to such dismissals.

IV. CONCLUSION

Because dismissal proceedings are, and should be, relatively infrequent, many institutions have had no direct experience with them. This inexperience contributes to the belief of many administrators, governing board members, and public spirited citizens that it can't be done; that a tenured professor simply cannot be dismissed for cause. The information presented should dispel that belief. The Study explained, analyzed and illustrated the concept of tenure and tenure's legal aspects, including the procedural and substantive legal dimensions of dismissals of tenured faculty members for cause. It has been demonstrated that nothing in either the concept of tenure, itself, or in its legal implementations that prevents, or unwarrantedly hampers, any institution from dismissing a tenured faculty member for (1) demonstrated incompetence or dishonesty in teaching or research; (2) substantial and manifest neglect of duty, including insubordination; or (3) personal conduct which substantially impairs the individual's fulfillment of his institutional responsibilities. Consequently, there is no cause for concern that institutions of higher education will be impaired in achieving their educational goals when, on January 1, 1994, mandatory age-based retirement policies become illegal.

There is little reason to expect a sudden surge of professional incompetency or neglect of duties by older professors where none existed previously. To the extent problems do develop among a few older, tenured professors who buck the trend toward earlier retirement and stay on, this Study, in Parts II and III, has demonstrated that the situations can be expeditiously handled by firm and humane administrators seeking a just and dignified resolution. Nothing in the concept of tenure or in its legal implementation precludes, or unwarrantedly interferes with, such resolutions, including the dismissal of tenured professors for cause after a tenure hearing proceeding where the grounds are fairly proved.

The burden of proof in establishing cause for dismissal of a tenured faculty member rests, and should rest, upon the institution. And, of course, institutions should "do it right." Many institutions have them, but *all* institutions need to have a tenure code setting forth *a set of fully adequate procedures* for the dismissal of tenured faculty members for cause. To that end, this Study, in Parts II and III, has set forth an analysis of the concept of tenure, descriptions and analyses of legal provisions and cases, plus recommended tenure code provisions and guidelines for additional provisions — all of which if faithfully followed, will enable institutions to produce fully adequate, age-neutral tenure codes, and "to do it right" in the event a dismissal proceeding is necessitated.

A. All Procedures Must Be Age-Neutral

It must be emphasized in any discussion of "uncapping," that whatever set of procedures an institution ultimately enacts, *it must be a set of procedures that is age-neutral.* The procedures can neither be aimed at older faculty members nor impact upon them disparately. The Age Discrimination In Employment Act (ADEA) described in the introduction to this Study applies to tenure and to other rules, regulations and decisions of private and public institutions of higher education. The ADEA, in 29 U.S.C. § 623(a), makes it "unlawful for an employer to fail or refuse to hire or to discharge any individual or otherwise discriminate against any individual with respect to his compensation, terms, conditions, or privileges of employment, because of such individual's age."

The bite of this provision is illustrated by *Leftwich v. Harris-Stowe College.*[181] The faculty member, Leftwich, of long and loyal service as a tenured professor of biology, lost his position when the state legislature transferred control for the college from a local board to the board of the state college system, with the college now having its own newly appointed board because it was legally considered to be a "new" college. The new board of the "new" college decided to hire only "new" and fewer faculty. However, under the plan a quota of tenured and nontenured faculty would be "newly hired" from the "old" college staff. There were two biology positions filled by a tenured and nontenured persons from the "old" college's staff. Leftwich was not hired, even though he scored higher on the Regents' evaluation measure than the two who were hired. Tenured faculty members who are older frequently command salaries that are higher than younger tenured or nontenured faculty members. Leftwich sued, alleging age discrimination, and the court agreed:[182]

> First, the record makes clear that the defendant's princi-
> pal, if not only, purpose in adopting their selection plan was
> to eliminate some tenure positions in order to effectuate
> cost savings. Second, to the extent that the defendants in
> fact utilized their selection plan in an attempt to increase the

---

[181] 702 F.2d 686 (6th Cir. 1983).
[182] *Id.* at 690-692.

quality of the college's faculty, they have failed to establish that the plan was necessary to achieve their goal . . . .

The defendants failed to demonstrate that reserving nontenured slots was necessary to bring new ideas to the college. Instead, their assertion that younger nontenured faculty would have new ideas apparently assumes that older tenured faculty members would cause the college to "stagnate." Such assumptions are precisely the kind of stereotypical thinking about older workers that the ADEA was designed to eliminate.

The appellate court ruled in favor of Leftwich. It awarded the professor a position on the "new" college faculty, retroactive seniority for the years missed because of his age-based discriminatory termination, back pay, attorney's fees, and court costs.

B. Involuntary versus Voluntary Termination

Observers suggest that about fifty cases of dismissal of tenured professors for cause arise each year in the United States, and well over half of them never go through the full tenure hearing process. Administrators should always be mindful that any policy of quick and ready resort to *involuntary* terminations of tenured faculty members, especially *involuntary* terminations of tenured faculty members having successful careers of long and loyal service, will create far more legal problems for an institution than the use of *voluntary* means for dissolving a tenured faculty member's relationship with an institution, because of the coercive and stigmatizing effects associated with dismissals for cause. Thus, as a simple matter of prudence that minimizes legal vulnerability and legal costs, not to mention the more important values involved, it is wise primarily to rely on *voluntary* alternatives to coercive dismissals for cause. But, of course, if they are not successful, then, as Parts II and III of this Study demonstrate, tenure creates no unwarranted obstacle to dismissals for cause.

Among voluntary methods available for inducing retirement of tenured faculty members are incentives of various kinds, including retirement counseling and "buy outs" which almost always are financially advantageous to an institution; the development of opportunities for phased or partial retirement such as teaching only one semester or quarter per academic year, and sponsorship of retraining for mid-career shifts to teaching and/or research in fields that are underpopulated. These inducements have proven themselves to be "cost effective." Imaginative creation of additional cost effective inducements for voluntary retirement is a field waiting to be plowed. The success of the alternatives depends on a thorough, fair and continuing review of personnel policies, coordinated planning by faculty and administration for future contingencies, and, of course, the careful and specific articulation of institutional policies in written documents, available to all. Yet, even in such circumstances, it is possible that resort to involuntary dismissal proceedings will be necessary.

Although related, but not strictly a part of the core concept of tenure itself, many institutions have some type of a pre-dismissal, pre-tenure-hearing procedure that makes considerable sense from the standpoints of institutional effectiveness and affording due process of law; that is, from the standpoints of dismissing incompetent faculty or those who substantially and manifestly neglect their duties, with fairness to both the faculty member and to the institution. The following pre-dismissal procedure is strongly recommended:[183]

> Dismissal of a faculty member with continuous tenure, or with a special or probationary appointment before the end of its specified term, first will be preceded: (1) by discussions between the faculty member and appropriate administrative officers looking toward a mutually fair and mutually advantageous and dignified settlement, and if unsuccessful then secondly (2) by informal inquiry by the democratic and duly elected committee of practicing academic faculty members with no administrators being eligible for service, and consisting of not less than five members [insert name here of committee other than that of the Tenure Hearing Committee] which shall review and evaluate all of the evidence supporting each charge against the faculty member and which committee after its review of the evidence shall seek to affect a dignified, mutually fair and mutually advantageous adjustment or settlement of the matter, meeting with all of the parties, separately or together, as often as necessary, but if in its judgment reached by consensus it has arrived at a deadend and is unsuccessful in its meetings with the parties, the committee shall then determine whether in its fully considered opinion dismissal proceedings should be undertaken, without its opinion being binding upon the president or other appropriate administrative or governing board officers, but delivering

---

[183] This recommendation is modelled after recommendation 5(b) found in the AAUP's 1982 Recommended Institutional Regulations on Academic Freedom and Tenure printed in ACADEME, p. 18a (Jan.-Feb. 1983).

its opinion on each charge, preferably by the whole committee, in its full detail and comprehensiveness on each charge and in a sensitive manner that, nevertheless, is quite candid and forthright, to the faculty member involved and to the appropriate administrative officer, almost always the president. The committee will continue to be available for further discussions with either the faculty member or the president so long as in the committee's judgment it can perform a useful role in the matter.

This procedure first involves initial and informal discussions between the faculty member and the administrative members of the institution which, may prove successful and produce agreement in a number of cases.

If the first step fails, then the second step in the procedure involves a committee composed of the faculty member's peers. The second step is advantageous to the institution and to the faculty member because it provides a dignified and respectful treatment of the issues from both viewpoints. The college or university is not precluded by the second step from proceeding to an ultimate tenure hearing, but before doing so, it first will have had the judgment of a group of independent faculty colleagues about the strength and persuasiveness of each charge in its case.

The second step in the recommended procedure is also advantageous to the charged faculty member, particularly when the burden of the evidence is against the faculty member, and particularly if his or her faculty colleagues on the committee are independent and well respected. But, to be advantageous to the charged professor, the committee members, preferably meeting collectively with the faculty member, must freely state their judgments about the scope and weight of the evidence quite candidly and unreservedly in their discussions. Such discussions and judgments will carry great weight when they come from non-adversarial, honest and respected faculty colleagues, rather than coming only administrators, who too easily can be perceived as adversaries having a special administrative goal to achieve at the expense of the faculty member.

In the circumstances envisioned by the second step of the proposed procedures and after full, perhaps repeated, discussions with colleagues, it is likely that when the evidence validates the charge in the judgment of their faculty colleagues on the committee, the overwhelming bulk of charged faculty members, and especially those beyond the age of seventy who have had dignified and successful careers, will elect to avoid a final, full-dress hearing. Coercive dismissals for cause clearly carry professional and social stigma. Almost all charged faculty members, especially older faculty members having had dignified, successful careers, will obviously desire to avoid such coercion and stigma. They will welcome the result most likely produced by the recommended procedure: a mutually fair and advantageous settlement which may well include their resignation in situations where the evidence is judged by their respected colleagues to be clearly against them.

To the extent that the few remaining tenured faculty members who may be charged with demonstrated incompetence or dishonesty, or substantial and manifest neglect of duty, might doggedly refuse the judgment of their peers on the pre-tenure-hearing committee and choose to proceed on to a full tenure hearing, there is nothing in the concept of tenure, itself, or in its legal implementation, as demonstrated in Parts II and III of this Study, that will protect the faculty member from dismissal if the charge is fairly validated by the evidence and if adequate due process procedures have been followed. Importantly, however, after following the recommended two-step procedure, and cases do progress to the final hearing, the morale of the rest of the institution's faculty members and the administrators should remain high. They will have the integrity produced by knowing of the honest care, concern and dignity sought to be preserved by an administration that has faithfully followed the first two steps, especially when it has done so in a way that conforms to the spirit as well as to the letter of the recommended provision.

One of the reasons accounting for the fact that comparatively few tenure hearings actually do occur is the considerable success of this kind of predismissal, pre-tenure-hearing procedure. It is recommended as a just, humane and dignified way for faculty members and institutions to resolve cases, especially cases involving faculty members aged 70 or more who have enjoyed successful careers, but who can validly be charged with (a) demonstrated incompetence or dishonesty or (b) substantial and manifest neglect of duty. Of all possible charges, these charges are the most likely ones to be brought against aged faculty members, although all cases may not necessarily be limited to them. Property used by institutional administrators and by faculty members, the preliminary two-step procedures set forth above may resolve the great bulk of any institution's potential cases.

C. The Need to Retain Older Faculty in the Coming Uncapped Academic World

In 1986, H.R. Bowen and J.H. Schuster projected a four percent faculty turnover rate by 1995.[184] Other researchers have predicted significant increases in the demand for new faculty members beginning as early as 1992. But, the facts are substantially different, for the future seems to have arrived earlier than expected. Findings in a recent Report of the American Council

---

[184] H.R. Bowen & J.H. Schuster, AMERICAN PROFESSORS: A NATIONAL RESOURCE IMPERILED (1986).

on Education[185] indicate that the turnover rate for full-time faculty members at the 364 colleges and universities surveyed was already at the five percent mark during academic year 1988-89. Ms. El-Khawas, who wrote the Report for ACE, stated that "the market now is absolutely turning"; that "this [Report] is seeming to say that the changes are happening sooner than the statistics told us about" and that "this is 1990 and things are changing."[186] The 1990 survey by the American Council on Education was the first to examine how institutions are responding to the changing academic labor market:[187]

> Responses varied among different types of institutions. For example, doctoral institutions were more likely than others to hire some faculty members, especially in high demand fields, at salaries above the institution's traditional scales. In the past year, more than half of the doctoral institutions surveyed have hired new junior faculty members at higher salaries than are paid to some senior professors in the same department.
>
> To make jobs more appealing, 9 in 10 institutions said they were taking steps to increase faculty compensation, while 6 in 10 were working to improve fringe benefits.

The Academic Personnel Annual Report 1988-1989, to the Assembly Of The Academic Senate Of The University of California states that "the University is expected to need 400 to 500 additional faculty members per year up to the year 2000 because of anticipated growth, including the projected new campuses. That expectation allows for an estimated 50% retirement of faculty members by 2000."[188] Presumably, the expectations of the University of California are not unique to that institution, although the magnitudes may be.

Many administrators have expressed the concern that "uncapping" would severely impact their *possibility* of hiring young or new faculty members, especially women and minorities, because with "uncapping" older faculty members would simply choose to stay on and occupy positions that otherwise could be used to hire young or new faculty members. But the fact of an existing five percent faculty turnover in 1989-90, which most likely will

---

[185] CAMPUS TRENDS, 1990, available for $13.00 per copy from ACE's Division Of Policy Analysis And Research, One Dupont Circle, Washington, D.C. (20036).

[186] Blum, *Job Market Begins Predicted Turnaround, Survey Indicates; Many Colleges Find It Impossible To Fill Faculty Vacancies*, 36 THE CHRON. OF HIGHER EDUC., A1, A11 (July 25, 1990).

[187] *Id.* at A12.

[188] Notice Of Meeting, Assembly of the Academic Senate, November 28, 1989.

continue during the 1990's, plus expansion due to increasing numbers of students, means that the expressed administrative concern about uncapping maybe wide of the mark.

Indeed, if the above quotes and the ACE Report constitute a true guide, the concerns of administrators now should be twofold: (1) how might they attract appealing young or new faculty members to careers in higher education when so many of them seem so disinclined to enter academia, and (2) how might they induce older faculty members to stay on, rather than voluntarily retire. Neither may be easy, because many faculty members, and those who would become faculty members, although upbeat, suffer from varying degrees of disenchantment with important aspects of academia. For example, a recent Survey and Report commissioned by the Carnegie Foundation For The Advancement Of Teaching,[189] found that of the 5,450 faculty members at 306 colleges and universities of all sizes that were consulted, 69% thought that the "administration at my institution is autocratic"; that 75% thought that "undergraduates are seriously underprepared," and that 67% thought that "standards in higher education are lower." Commenting on the Carnegie Foundation Report's findings, Ernest L. Boyer, President of the Carnegie Foundation said, "We cannot overstate our urgency about the problems faculty have defined."[190] Faculty members sense a disturbing and widening gulf between professors and their students, and between professors and administrators:[191]

> Said Mr. Boyer: "There's a growing gap between the faculty culture and the student culture." Many professors, he added, feel their students are interested in acquiring knowledge only to help them reach career goals as efficiently as possible. "They only want to know the rules — 'Tell us the formula,'" he said. "It's a credentialing process and not a process of education."
>
> Nearly two-thirds of the full-time professors, meanwhile, rated the administration at their institutions as "fair" or "poor." More than two-thirds — slightly more than in 1984 — also felt their administrations were "autocratic," although faculty members at liberal-arts colleges were more likely to view their administrations as "democratic."

---

[189] THE CONDITION OF THE PROFESSORATE: ATTITUDES AND TRENDS, 1989, available for $12.00 per copy from Princeton University Press.

[190] Reported in Mooney, *Professors Are Upbeat About Profession But Uneasy About Students Standards*, 36 THE CHRON. OF HIGHER EDUC. A1, A18 (November 8, 1989).

[191] *Id.*

Mr. Boyer suggested that many professors held negative views of campus leadership because they felt that as their institutions had grown and become more complex, they had failed to provide their faculty members with sufficient opportunity to participate in the changes.

Other publications show that more and more tenured faculty members are complaining, dissatisfied that they effectively are being turned into private entrepreneurs by the growing, at times severe, pressures placed upon them by their institutions to compete successfully for grant monies, which not only will pay their salaries and collateral benefits, but also will yield an additional sum for use by the college or university.

D. The Role of Academic Tenure in the 1990's

A robustly healthy system of academic tenure benefits the institution, faculty members, and society. Tenure may be helpful to administrators not only as they recruit young faculty members to academic life but also as they seek to retain older ones.

As identified in this Study, tenure is the essential condition of academic freedom, and academic freedom is the *sine qua non* requirement for effectiveness as a faculty member. The existence of a robustly healthy system of tenure and academic freedom on a campus creates an atmosphere favorable to all faculty members, whether tenured or not, because the independence afforded the tenured faculty members enables them to form an independent body capable of protecting their academic freedom and that of their non-tenured colleagues. Moreover, by creating a faculty with a long-term commitment to the college or university, tenure makes its contributions to institutional stability, loyalty, esprit, collegiality and to effective institutional governance.

Tenure demands that institutional decisions about professional competence and responsibility be made on professional grounds, and not on grounds of competitive advantage. A robustly healthy system of academic tenure consistently encourages faculty members to be faithful to its ideals and to concentrate on their fundamental academic obligations to students and to advancing the intellectual content of their disciplines, thereby attracting men and women of ability into the profession, while simultaneously minimizing competition solely for economic advantage. Tenure's severe "up-or-out" requirement promotes the creation of faculties of truly outstanding persons, rather than merely agreeable persons who have been kept on because of friendship, generosity or neglect. Finally, another "advantage" of tenure must be faced: it has a long-term economic value that helps to counteract the generally lower financial rewards of higher education, thereby enabling colleges and universities to compete in fields where they otherwise would be shut out — not only in medicine or law, but also in physics, mathematics, chemistry, engineering, economics, business, psychology and many other fields which currently have highly developed markets in society at large. As the Harvard Committee On Governance concluded after examining the history of "intellectual and curricular" innovation at Harvard:[192]

> It is observably the case that most of the major experimental changes in Harvard education — the "case system" at the law and business schools; the interdisciplinary programs such as comparative literature and American civilization in the Graduate School of Arts and Sciences; and a long series of developments in the colleges, from the creation (in the waning years of the Eliot elective system) of history and literature as an undergraduate interdisciplinary honors concentration to the formulation and launching of general education — have derived from the thinking, the time and the energies of tenured faculty members.

Given that academic tenure has proven itself to be such a venerable and highly useful institution to higher education in this country, this Study concludes that academic tenure will continue to make its contributions to the future of academic life in America's institutions of higher education because there is no need to modify it due to the ADEA's prohibition on January 1, 1994, of age-based mandatory retirement policies. This Study also concludes that there is no need to modify the ADEA's prospective prohibition of mandatory age-based retirement either due to the concept of tenure or due to its legal implementation, because tenure poses no substantial hindrance to institutions of higher education in an "uncapped" context; instead, academic tenure provides a ready, proven and effective means of continuing to help institutions of higher education realize their purposes and goals in the future "uncapped" academic world.

---

[192] Discussion Memorandum on Academic Tenure At Harvard University, 17 (1971), *quoted in* W. Keast and J.W. Macy, Jr., *Commission On Academic Tenure In The United States*, Faculty Tenure, 18 (1973) (italics in original).

APPENDIX

Dismissal Procedure Guidelines

(1)   A dismissal will be preceded by a statement of definite reasons and specific, clear charge(s) which will be specifically and definitely stated, and related, directly and substantially, to the fitness of faculty members in their professional capacities as teachers researchers (see 3 below), and the individual concerned will have the right to be heard initially by the democratically elected faculty hearing committee [insert name of the Tenure Hearing Committee here] composed of currently tenured professors without administrative appointments. Committee members deeming themselves disqualified for bias or interest will remove themselves from the case, either at the request of a party or on their own initiative. Each party will have a maximum of two challenges to Committee members without stating any cause.

(2)   The hearing committee may, with the consent of the parties concerned, hold joint prehearing meetings with the parties in order to (i) simplify the issues, (ii) effect stipulations of facts, (iii) provide for the exchange of documentary or other information, and (iv) achieve such other appropriate pre-hearing objectives as will make the hearing fair, effective, and expeditious.

(3)   Service of notice of hearing with specific charges in writing will be made at least twenty days prior to the hearing. The faculty member may waive a hearing or may respond to the charges in writing at any time before the hearing. If the faculty member waives a hearing, but denies the charges or asserts that the charges do not support a finding of adequate cause, the hearing tribunal will evaluate all available evidence and rest its recommendation upon the evidence in the record.

(4)   The committee, in consultation with the president and the faculty member, will exercise its judgment as to whether the hearing should be public or private.

(5)   During the proceedings the faculty member will be permitted to have an academic advisor and counsel of the faculty member's choice.

(6)   At the request of either party or the hearing committee, a representative of a responsible educational association will be permitted to attend the proceedings as an observer.

(7)   A verbatim record of the hearing or hearings will be taken and a typewritten copy will be made available to the faculty member as soon as possible and without cost, at the faculty member's request.

(8)   The burden of proof that adequate cause exists rests with the institution and will be satisfied only by clear and convincing evidence in the record considered as a whole.

(9)   The hearing committee will grant adjournments to enable either party to investigate evidence as to which a valid claim of surprise is made.

(10)   The faculty member will be afforded an opportunity to obtain necessary witnesses and documentary or other evidence. The administration will cooperate with the hearing committee in securing witnesses and making available documentary and other evidence.

(11)   The faculty member and the administration will have the right to confront and cross-examine all witnesses. Where the witnesses cannot or will not appear, but the committee determines that the interests of justice require admission of their statements, the committee will identify the witnesses, disclose their statements, and if possible provide for interrogatories.

(12)   In the hearing of charges of incompetence, the testimony will include that of qualified faculty members from this or other institutions of higher education.

(13)   The hearing committee will not be bound by strict rules of legal evidence, and may admit any evidence which is of probative value in determining the issues involved; however, the receipt of hearsay evidence should be limited, and every possible effort will be made to obtain the most reliable evidence available in every instance.

(14)   The findings of fact and the decision will be based solely on the hearing record.

(15)   Except for such simple announcements as may be required, covering the time of the hearing and similar matters, public statements and publicity about the case by either the faculty member or administrative officers will be avoided so far as possible until the proceedings have been completed, including consideration by the president and/or governing board of the institution. The president and the faculty member will be notified of the decision in writing and will be given a copy of the record of the hearing.

(16) If the hearing committee concludes that adequate cause for dismissal has not been established by the evidence in the record, it will so report to the president. If the president rejects the report, the president will state the reasons for doing so, in writing, to the hearing committee and to the faculty member, and provide an opportunity for response before transmitting the case to the governing board. If the hearing committee concludes that adequate cause for a dismissal has been established, but that an academic penalty less than dismissal would be more appropriate, it will so recommend, with supporting reasons.

Final Action by the Governing Board

If dismissal or other severe sanction is recommended the president will, on request of the faculty member, transmit to the governing board the record of the case. The governing board's review will be based on the record of the committee hearing, and it will provide opportunity for argument, oral or written or both, by the principals at the hearings or by their representatives. The decision of the hearing committee will either be sustained, or the proceeding will be returned to the committee with specific objections. The committee will then reconsider, taking into account the stated objections and receiving new evidence if necessary. The governing board thereafter will make a final decision only after study of the committee's reconsideration Dismissal Procedure Guidelines.

TABLE OF CASES

INDEX